The Internet with Vista
for the
Older Generation

Other Books of Interest

* * * * *

Acknowledgements

The author and publishers would like to thank the following for their help in the preparation of this book:

HBOS plc for kindly providing Halifax plc and Bank of Scotland information. The National Archives, Kew (formerly the Public Record Office) for permission to reproduce extracts from the 1901 Census Online. Michael Dibben, The Tarbert Hotel, Penzance, Cornwall. Mark Gatenby, The Gatenbys of Yorkshire Web Site.

The Internet with Vista for the Older Generation

Jim Gatenby

BERNARD BABANI (publishing) LTD
The Grampians
Shepherds Bush Road
London W6 7NF
England

www.babanibooks.com

Please Note

Although every care has been taken with the production of this book to ensure that any projects, designs, modifications and/or programs, etc., contained herewith, operate in a correct and safe manner and also that any components specified are normally available in Great Britain, the Publishers and Author do not accept responsibility in any way for the failure (including fault in design) of any project, design, modification or program to work correctly or to cause damage to any equipment that it may be connected to or used in conjunction with, or in respect of any other damage or injury that may be so caused, nor do the Publishers accept responsibility in any way for the failure to obtain specified components.

Notice is also given that if equipment that is still under warranty is modified in any way or used or connected with home-built equipment then that warranty may be void.

© 2007 BERNARD BABANI (publishing) LTD

First Published - September 2007

British Library Cataloguing in Publication Data:

A catalogue record for this book is available from the
British Library

ISBN 978 085934 615 3
Cover Design by Gregor Arthur
Printed and bound in Great Britain by Cox and Wyman Ltd

About this Book

This book is a companion to the best-selling title, The Internet for the Older Generation. This new book includes the many innovative features of Windows Vista and Internet Explorer 7, while The Internet for the Older Generation is still available for users of Windows XP, etc. Like other books in the highly successful Older Generation series, this book attempts to show, in plain English and avoiding technical jargon, that older people in particular have much to gain by using the Internet.

The first chapter outlines some of the many ways the Internet can help with daily life. The next chapter gives advice on setting up an Internet computer in your home and explains the technical jargon used by the computer trade.

Windows Vista introduces many new features affecting the way we interact with the computer and these are described in detail, together with help for users with special needs including speech recognition. The process of connecting to the Internet is described, with advice on choosing an Internet Service Provider and discussion of the latest high speed *broadband* services, including Wi-Fi home networks.

The highly-praised Internet Explorer 7 Web "browser" is discussed in detail. A chapter is devoted to Windows Mail, the new e-mail program included in Windows Vista. Using the popular Google program to search for all sorts of information is explained, together with Internet activities such as arranging holidays, home banking and security.

Importing digital photographs from various sources is also covered, together with e-mailing photos directly from the Windows Photo Gallery. This includes compressing photographs to speed up transfer across the Internet. The final chapter looks at different methods of creating your own simple Web site including free, easy-to-use software.

About the Author

Jim Gatenby trained as a Chartered Mechanical Engineer and initially worked at Rolls-Royce Ltd using early computers in the analysis of aircraft engine performance. He obtained a Master of Philosophy degree in Mathematical Education by research and taught mathematics and computing to students of all ages for many years, including the well-established CLAIT computer literacy course. Since retiring from teaching he has written many books involving computing and Microsoft Windows. These include several of the popular Older Generation series from Bernard Babani (publishing) Ltd, and in particular the best-selling book Computing for the Older Generation.

Trademarks

Microsoft, MSN, Hotmail, Windows, Windows Vista, Windows Aero, Windows XP, Windows Media Player, Windows Mail and Internet Explorer are either trademarks or registered trademarks of Microsoft Corporation. Norton AntiVirus and Norton 360 are trademarks of Symantec Corporation. Paint Shop Pro is a trademark or registered trademark of Corel Corporation. Google and Blogger are trademarks or registered trademarks of Google Inc. Adobe Photoshop and Adobe Photoshop Elements are trademarks of Adobe Systems Incorporated. F-Secure Internet Security is a trademark or registered trademark of F-Secure Corporation. Yahoo! and GeoCities are trademarks or registered trademarks of Yahoo! Inc. WebPlus is a trademark of Serif (Europe) Ltd.

All other brand and product names used in this book are recognized as trademarks or registered trademarks, of their respective companies.

Contents

1

2

3

4

5

11

12

13

Why Use the Internet?

You're Never Too Old

Television and the media often report on the amazing computing exploits of youngsters – "whiz-kids" who demonstrate impressive skills and knowledge. As a result many older people may wrongly feel excluded from this exciting new world. Such prowess among the young is hardly surprising since many children are growing up with computers in their bedrooms and also using the machines all day at school. Many of us older people had to manage with pen and ink and before that chalk and slates! So naturally some older people are fearful of getting started with the new technology and probably think they've missed the boat. This is a pity because the Internet can greatly improve the way people of all ages communicate and enable them to find information on any conceivable subject under the sun – and not just technical stuff.

A friend of mine, Arthur, is 75 years young and living proof that age is no barrier to becoming confident and skilled in computing and the Internet, as shown on the next page.

In a typical week Arthur might:

- Build a new computer to a customer's requirements.
- Repair several machines, upgrade some others and install the latest Windows Vista software.
- Set up some broadband Internet connections.
- "Download" music tracks and video and save them on a CD or DVD.

Of course, not everyone wants to get involved in the technical aspects of computing like Arthur. However, you can still use computers and the Internet to enrich your daily life in many different ways. A big advantage for older people is that in later life there's often more time to learn new skills at a leisurely pace, without the pressures of a full-time job or looking after a family.

Anyone Can Use a Modern Computer

Tremendous efforts have been made in recent years to make computers easy to use. There's no longer any need to learn complicated commands or technical jargon. If you were put off computing years ago because it was so complex, now is a good time to forget your past experience and make a fresh start. These days nearly everything can be

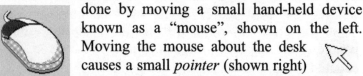

done by moving a small hand-held device known as a "mouse", shown on the left. Moving the mouse about the desk causes a small *pointer* (shown right) to move across the screen. To carry out a task, the pointer is moved over a word or a small picture (*icon*) representing the task and a button (usually the left-hand one) is pressed on the mouse.

It's easier than navigating the teletext menus on a television!

Help for People with Special Needs

If you're worried about physical impairments such as failing eyesight or mobility, the latest Windows Vista computer system has built-in help, known as *Ease of Access* features. These include a *magnifier* to display an enlargement of the text on the screen. There is also an *on-screen keyboard* operated by the mouse, for anyone who finds a conventional keyboard difficult to use.

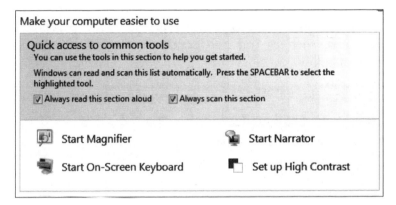

Help for users with special needs is covered in more detail later in this book.

The Diversity of the Internet

The next few pages attempt to give a taste of the vast range of activities now possible with the Internet, appealing to people of all ages and interests. Some of these topics are covered in more detail later in this book.

In the business world, few modern companies are without a "Web site". This is usually several pages of text and pictures about the organization. Web pages are posted up on special computers all over the world, known as *Web servers*.

1   Why Use the Internet?

Millions of computers in homes, schools and offices can be connected to the Internet to view Web pages from anywhere in the world. As shown later, it's a simple matter for ordinary people to create their own personal Web site to share their interests.

Many small businesses have seen their sales take off after getting a Web site which allows orders to be placed and paid for "online". A recent report announced that most of the farms in Britain are now connected to the Internet, enabling them to advertise their produce and to promote activities such as bed and breakfast accommodation, as shown below.

Thistleyhaugh is a picturesque Georgian farmhouse situated on the banks of the River Coquet near Alnwick, Rothbury and Morpeth in the heart of rural Northumberland.

Obtaining Information on Any Subject

School children have been using the Internet to research homework topics for some years. However, older people can also benefit from this enormous store of knowledge. You can find out about any subject, such as health, holidays, gardening, sport and news. For example, you can get the latest information on medical conditions, compiled by doctors and also including contributions from patients.

Education Online

You can learn new subjects *online* under schemes such as Learndirect. Anyone can obtain first-class educational materials by *downloading* them. This means copying *files* such as text, graphics, photographs, music, video or software from an Internet *server*, then saving the files on the internal hard disc of your own computer.

Keeping In Touch With Friends and Family

E-mails are text messages which can also include pictures, sent around the world, between computers and other devices. Various files or *attachments* such as photographs, documents and video clips can be appended to an e-mail. If the recipient reads their mail regularly, communication can be almost instantaneous anywhere in the world. Inexpensive cameras, or *webcams*, together with a cheap microphone, allow you to speak with people and see them in "real-time". In business this is known as *video conferencing*; in a family context it might, for example, allow someone to use their computer in England to speak with and see their grandchildren in Australia.

Researching Your Family History

Huge databases on the Internet such as the 1901 Census allow us to trace our ancestors and build up a family tree.

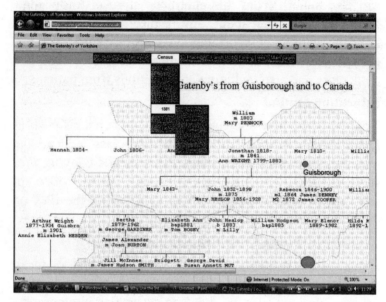

Some Web sites allow you to post up notices asking for information about long-lost relatives. These can be seen by millions of people anywhere the world and often lead to rewarding contacts. This can start a dialogue carried out across the world by e-mail and may result in reunions of long-lost friends and families. There are also many Web sites listing parish records and giving advice and help in compiling family trees. This subject is covered in more detail later in this book.

Internet Shopping

Online shopping allows you to browse catalogues and purchase books, groceries, music, etc., from the comfort of your own home. Major supermarkets such as Tesco and Sainsbury have built up significant online shopping enterprises, saving you the time and effort of the weekly shopping trip.

After completing your initial order online (in only a few minutes), the system "remembers" your shopping list and this can be used as the basis for your future weekly shopping. In subsequent weeks you only have to select any new items and confirm or omit the items on your basic list. Online shopping can literally reduce an entire week's shopping to just a few minutes at the computer.

Hotel Accommodation

Many hotels and other providers of holidays allow you to view the accommodation and check vacancies on your screen before making a reservation online. Some Web sites provide a *virtual tour* or a short video guide around the accommodation. To find out more about the surrounding area, there are now webcams in many resorts giving panoramic views, updated every few minutes.

Unlike the conventional holiday brochure, the information on the Web site should be absolutely up-to-date; requests for further information and bookings can be dealt with immediately. Once connected to the Internet, you can *immediately* find holiday information for destinations anywhere in the world – you don't have to wait while brochures are sent to you by the traditional post.

Internet Banking

Internet Bank accounts can be opened, usually offering a higher rate of interest than conventional accounts in High Street branches. Most of the normal banking services are available online, such as transferring money between accounts, setting up standing orders, paying bills and ordering holiday currency to be delivered to your home.

Obtaining Music and Software

An enormous range of music, video clips and computer software can be downloaded, i.e. transferred from the Internet and saved on your own computer. You can download a whole album or just a single track. It's often possible to play a short sample of a track before deciding to add it to your virtual shopping basket. After you've completed your shopping, payment is made by entering your card details before clicking a button to start the download. This only takes a few minutes with a broadband connection. You can use your downloaded music to "burn" your own CDs. With a suitable printer and "printable" CDs, labels and artwork can be printed on the top of the CD.

Making Your Own Web Site

At one time, creating a Web site was a very complicated affair and involved step-by step instructions which you typed into the computer. These instructions had to be "coded" in a special language called HTML or HyperText Markup Language. Like many computing activities, creating a Web site has been simplified by easy-to-use software which virtually does the job for you. Various page creation software packages exist, such as Serif's WebPlus, a powerful yet easy-to-use program. The Yahoo! GeoCities Web site provides free software tools online, including ready-made designs and templates – all you do is enter your own text for the Web pages.

Creating a Blog

The *blog* (short for "Weblog") is probably the quickest and easiest way to establish your presence on the Internet. A blog is simply an online diary or journal which can be viewed worldwide and into which you can "post" regular entries. A blog service such as Blogger provides all the necessary tools free, including ready-made page designs into which you type your news, etc., and add any pictures.

The Virtual Auction

You might want to get rid of a lot of household clutter acquired over the years, or maybe you are "downsizing" to a smaller property. (Or perhaps you just need to raise some cash.) An online auction site like *eBay* may provide the answer to getting rid of your unwanted chattels. The range of goods sold on eBay is enormous, from antiques and collectables, music, travel and tickets to cars and spare parts. The advantage to the seller is that you gain access to a worldwide marketplace of millions of potential customers. eBay has been so successful that, apart from ordinary people disposing of a few unwanted items, many people are making a full-time living out of online selling. Many traditional businesses also use eBay to vastly increase their potential market.

The online auction is similar to the traditional sale in that the buyer has to bid for an item and the seller sets a minimum or reserve price. A major difference is that online bids are placed over a limited period of time, decided by the seller, typically several days. At the end of the time period, the item is sold to the highest bidder, who must pay for the goods before the seller arranges delivery by conventional postage. The online auction site publishes satisfaction ratings of sellers, based on previous customers' experiences.

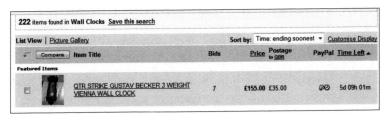

One Family's Use of the Internet

Then following is a list of some of the ways my own family have used the Internet over the last few years; most of these tasks would take much longer by traditional methods and some would probably be impossible:

- Booked holidays after checking current vacancies, including a 3-D virtual tour of the accommodation and Web Cam views of the surrounding area.

- Found up-to-date information about illnesses.

- Ordered the weekly shopping in a few minutes online, delivered to the door, saving time and avoiding the stress of supermarket shopping.

- Used a family Web site to trace and renew contact with long-lost cousins in England and Canada; received messages and photos. Printed a family tree.

- Used the 1901 Online Census to find details of relatives alive at that time, including addresses, occupations and other household members.

- Ordered books online, delivered the next day.

- Viewed 5-day weather forecast for holidays.

- Printed airline pilot's monthly flight roster.

- Tracked flight arrivals and departures.

- Checked in online, avoiding airport queuing.

- Researched Inheritance Tax and ways to avoid it.

- Received, as e-mail attachments, draft copies of Wills for checking, saving considerable time.

- Used a Wi-Fi laptop at hotels and airports to find information from the Internet and read e-mails.

- Validated the ownership history and checked the book value of a second-hand car.

- Received examination results online at midnight, over a day before the paper copy arrived in the post.

- "Downloaded" software and music of all types from the Internet and saved it on a home computer.

- Found information about plants, shrubs and gardening equipment. Tracked down elusive greenhouse spare parts, otherwise unobtainable.

- Opened an Internet bank account offering an above-average interest rate. Checked statements, set up standing orders and transferred funds online.

- Searched for and found a suitable flat in Edinburgh.

- Used the RSPB Web site to identify garden birds and view their characteristics, including samples of their songs and videos of the birds in flight.

Summary – Why Use the Internet?

The purpose of this chapter was to try to show that older people have much to gain by using computers and the Internet. No-one need worry about the supposed difficulty of learning new computing skills; modern systems have been designed and tested to make sure they are easy for normal people to use. Most tasks just require you to "point and click" at simple instructions and menus on the screen.

If you find physical tasks difficult for any reason, there are various Ease of Access features built into Windows Vista. These features are intended to help people having common impairments and are described in more detail in Chapter 4.

Forget the popular image of the Internet as a plaything for young "whiz-kids" trying to "hack" into banks and military installations or spread deadly computer viruses. As listed earlier in this chapter and described in more detail later in this book, there is a multitude of worthwhile, sensible uses of the Internet, from which older people can benefit greatly. With the extra time often available in later life, the Internet can become a mentally stimulating and rewarding hobby. Also, as many older people (including myself) have found, computing and the Internet can be the starting point for an interesting new career or small business.

After reading this book (and perhaps the companion volume "Computing with Vista for the Older Generation" from Bernard Babani (publishing) Ltd), you may wish to join one of the many computing courses. The popular CLAIT scheme covers most aspects of computer use including the Internet. These courses are held at local adult education centres, often with a choice of either daytime or evening sessions. Such courses are usually very friendly and supportive, allowing you to progress at your own rate.

Getting Set Up

Choosing a Location in Your Home

The ideal place for your computer is a small room which can be used as a dedicated office, with few distractions, especially if you're aiming to get down to some serious work. I converted part of our garage into an office, as shown below. A special computer desk was bought for a song from a local supplier of second-hand office furniture. Office furniture is usually more robust and of superior quality to the equivalent items designed for the home user.

Far from heralding the "paperless office", computers seem to increase the amount of paperwork. In my experience, if you're doing any sort of office work you can't have too much desk space. This can be maximized by using one of the latest flat-screen monitors and by placing the main computer tower unit on the floor as shown below. A cordless mouse and keyboard further reduce clutter.

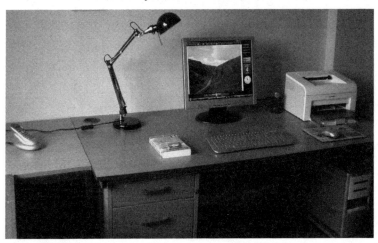

Safety and Security

Computers are very popular with thieves, so try to make sure your system is not clearly visible from outside. If you choose to base your computer in a garden shed or other outbuilding, make sure it's secure and not damp.

A modern computer system including all of the peripheral devices such as a printer and a scanner can easily require six or more power points. For safety reasons you should not overload your power points or have a "bird's nest" of wires trailing all over the floor. It may be advisable to have some extra power points installed and certified by a qualified electrician. Faulty wiring might invalidate insurance policies in the event of a fire.

Connecting to a Telephone Line

Your computer will need to be connected to a telephone socket in order to access the Internet and send and receive e-mails and information from Web sites. Depending on the type of Internet connection you choose, this may mean that you will not be able to use the telephone at the same time as the Internet. This subject is discussed in more detail later, but a brief explanation follows.

The Dial-Up Modem

Traditionally computers have been connected to the telephone lines by a device known as the *dial-up modem*; this literally has to dial a telephone number to connect to an Internet server computer. Many people have replaced their dial-up modems with much faster *broadband systems* discussed shortly.

The modem is a small electronic device used to convert between the digital data of the computer and the analogue (sound) data transmitted by the telephone lines.

The modem connects to the telephone line through an adaptor with two sockets. A cable from the computer via the modem connects into one socket, while the ordinary telephone handset is plugged into the other socket. When you're online to the Internet (using a dial-up modem), you can't use the telephone at the same time.

Installing a Separate Telephone Line

One rather expensive solution to the above problem is to have a separate telephone line installed, dedicated to the Internet. With a separate telephone line for the Internet you can be billed separately for your Internet telephone charges, as distinct from your normal household telephone bill. This would be helpful if your Internet connection is used for business and you can set your Internet telephone charges against profits, for tax purposes.

Broadband Connection

The latest method of connecting to the Internet is called *broadband* and works very much faster than the dial-up modem.

- Unlike the dial-up modem, which literally has to dial-up a telephone number every time you go online, broadband normally stays connected to the Internet all day.

- The extra speed of broadband makes it much quicker to find and display Web pages and to download music, video and software, etc.

- A major advantage is that broadband allows the Internet and an ordinary telephone handset to be used at the same time on a single telephone line.

In some very isolated areas broadband may not be available without the installation of special equipment.

Choosing a Computer System

Most computers sold to both home and business users are known as *PCs*, after the original IBM Personal Computer. In fact there are thousands of manufacturers of PCs ranging from one-man local businesses to large international corporations. Most of these PC machines use the Microsoft Windows operating system (of which Windows Vista is the latest version). The operating system controls the screen display and the entire running of the computer. The user interacts with the operating system using a mouse and a series of rectangular boxes or "windows" on the screen. Shown below is a window containing the Windows Vista **Control Panel**. This is used for altering the computer's settings and adding and removing software and hardware.

The background behind the **Control Panel** above is known as the **Windows Desktop**. The *icons* or small pictures in the **Control Panel** window (and on the Desktop behind) are double-clicked to launch programs, tools and open folders.

On-screen menus as well as *icons* are pointed to and clicked with the mouse to launch a particular task. The windows, icons, menus and pointer are known as a *WIMP* system and also as a *graphical user interface (GUI)*.

The PC has become the world-wide standard for home and business computers and has generated a huge amount of software. There is also plenty of support for the PC, including spare parts and small local businesses experienced in carrying out repairs and upgrades to keep the machines up-to-date.

Nowadays the only serious alternative to the Windows PC is the Apple Macintosh, in various forms. The Apple Mac has many devoted users since it was the pioneer of easy-to-use mouse and windows operating systems. The Mac has established itself as the preferred choice in many printing and publishing enterprises and in some areas of education.

For the general user wishing to remain in the mainstream of readily-available software, cheap hardware and support, there is really no choice other than to buy a PC machine running Microsoft Windows Vista.

Choosing a Supplier

If buying from a small local computer shop, try to find a business that has been around for a few years and is recommended by satisfied customers. If there are any problems, you can take your machine back to the person who built it. In the case of the large supplier, your computer may need to be sent away for repair and may not be seen again for several weeks. Fortunately modern computers are usually very reliable and you'll probably have no problems. The small local business will often build a computer to your own specification as discussed shortly.

Suggested Questions for Computer Suppliers

So that you won't be "blinded with science" at the computer shop, it should help if you do some preparation for your visit. You might prepare a list of questions – a good supplier will have no problem in giving you honest answers. A few ideas are given below.

- What system would best suit my intended use of the computer?

- Is it easy to upgrade the computer in the future, with more memory, faster processor, bigger hard disc, more expansion cards?

- What guarantee is included with the machine and what does it cover?

- What are the arrangements for returning the machine and who pays for transportation?

- What is a typical turnaround time for repairs?

- What software is pre-installed on the machine – Windows Vista, word processor, spreadsheet, etc?

- What peripherals are included – printer, scanner, digital camera, etc?

- Would the basic machine without these "free" peripherals be better value? Also, you may want a better printer, for example, than the one included in a particular package.

- Will the supplier deliver the computer and get it up and running in your home, including connecting to the Internet?

After buying a new machine, keep all receipts and packaging in case the system has to be returned for repair.

Buying a New Computer

Perfectly adequate new PC machines suitable for accessing the Internet can be bought from the large retailers for under £400 including VAT, at the time of writing. Machines with increased performance may cost upwards of £500. Such a machine will typically have more *memory*, faster *processor*, bigger *hard disc drive*, etc. If you don't understand such computer jargon, these terms are explained shortly and in the Glossary at the end of this book. However, for general Internet use, e.g. finding information from Web pages, creating your own Web site, downloading files and using e-mail, a £400 machine will be quite powerful enough.

When buying a new computer, choose one with Vista Home Premium edition already installed if you want to get the entire Vista experience, including the Windows Aero graphics discussed shortly.

Second-Hand Machines

Computers depreciate very rapidly and you can pick up a decent used machine quite cheaply. In fact, at the time of writing, one local computer builder is selling refurbished machines for £100; these should be quite capable of general Internet use, although it may be necessary to upgrade them to run Windows Vista. Checking an older machine for readiness to run Windows Vista is covered at the end of this chapter.

Carrying out the necessary upgrades and modifications to enable an older machine to run Vista is described in our book "Computing with Vista for the Older Generation" from Bernard Babani (publishing) Ltd.

The Computer Specification

It's a good idea to make yourself familiar with the main computer components before you visit suppliers to talk about a purchase; then an unscrupulous sales person won't be able to blind you with science. Here's a typical specification for a PC from a large retailer:

> - Intel Pentium 3.2GHz Processor
> - 1GB RAM
> - 160GB Hard Drive
> - DVD and CD-Rewriter Drives
> - 17-inch TFT Monitor
> - 128MB GeForce Graphics
> - Windows Vista Home Premium
> - £399.99 including VAT

The above specification contains a lot of computer jargon. Each of the above terms is explained on the next few pages.

Windows Vista requires quite a powerful machine to run at its full potential. A machine of the specification listed above will be quite capable of running Windows Vista.

However, if you already have an older machine, it may be possible to upgrade it to run Vista by replacing some of the critical components such as the memory, processor, graphics card and hard disc drive. These issues are discussed in more detail in the remainder of this chapter and in our companion book in this series "Computing with Vista for the Older Generation" from Bernard Babani (publishing) Ltd.

The Jargon Explained

Microsoft Windows Vista

The Microsoft Windows operating system is dominant on personal computers throughout the world. The Windows system enables you to "drive" the computer using a mouse and a series of on-screen menus and icons which represent different tasks and programs. The screen is divided up into one or more "windows" or frames.

Windows Vista is the latest version of Microsoft Windows. There are four versions including two aimed at the home user; these are Vista Home Basic, the cheapest, and Vista Home Premium. Home Premium is the best choice for the home user, as it has many advanced graphics features, greatly enhancing your use of the computer.

Windows Vista includes **Internet Explorer 7**; this is a program known as a *Web browser*, allowing you to find and display Web pages and save and print copies. Internet Explorer 7 is described in detail later in this book.

The Processor

This is the "brains" of the computer. It's a micro-chip which carries out all of the high-speed instructions and calculations. The Intel Pentium is probably the most well-known brand of processor, but there are rivals such as the AMD Athlon and Duron processors. Currently *dual core* processors are very popular; these have two processors mounted on a single chip.

"3.2GHz" in the previous specification refers to the speed the processor carries out instructions. Until recently I was still using a 1GHz machine and this was quite adequate for general Internet use. So the 3.2GHz processor listed in the specification on the previous page should be good for several years before it's rendered obsolete by the march of technological progress.

MHz or megahertz is a measure of the speed of the processor in millions of instructions per second.

1GHz or gigahertz is roughly 1000 megahertz.

DVD and CD-Rewriter Drives

These are devices built into your computer which allow you to copy music, video and data files onto blank CDs and DVDs, including files you have downloaded from the Internet. The CDs and DVDs can then be used in ordinary players, away from the computer. Music and video can also be copied from CDs and DVDs and stored on your computer's hard disc drive. They can then be accessed easily and played with the Windows Media Player, which is included with Window Vista.

The RAM

RAM stands for *Random Access Memory*. It is a *temporary store* in the computer and holds the programs and data currently being used. 1GB is a measure of the storage capacity of the RAM. 1GB is fast becoming the norm on computers running Windows Vista, while some people have already decided that 2GB is really needed.

1GB or gigabyte is approximately 1000MB.

1MB is approximately 1 million bytes.

A byte is the amount of memory needed to store a character such as a letter of the alphabet or a number 0-9.

The terms bytes, kilobytes, megabytes and gigabytes refer to the storage capacity of the memory (RAM) and media such as hard discs, CDs and DVDs, etc. The sizes of files to be downloaded from the Internet are also quoted in kilobytes and megabytes. Such files might include photographs, music, video and software updates. The RAM is said to be *volatile* memory; data and programs stored in the RAM are lost when the computer is switched off.

Saving Permanently

Programs and data must be saved permanently by recording on the computer's internal hard disc and on removable media such as CDs, DVDs, and the latest *flash drives* also known as *pen drives*, *memory sticks* and *removable discs*. These are small devices in the form of *dongles* which plug into the rectangular USB ports on the computer.

Flash drive dongle   **USB Ports**

The Hard Disc Drive

The *hard disc drive* (also called the *hard disc* and *the hard drive*) consists of several magnetic metal discs on a central spindle, rotating at high speed. The hard disc is enclosed in a metal casing and mounted inside of the main case of your computer. The hard disc is your computer's virtual filing cabinet in which all of your programs and data files (such as word processing documents) are permanently stored. The Windows Vista operating system and its many associated files also occupy a considerable amount of the hard disc space. The hard disc can also be used to save your e-mails and any Web pages and files downloaded from the Internet.

160GB in the previous specification is a good size hard disc – in fact it's phenomenal compared with the size of hard disc drives of a few years ago. Such a hard disc will be more than adequate for the general computer user.

As can be seen from the screenshot below, the machine I am currently using has a relatively modest 68.5GB hard disc, of which 27.6GB are still unused. The hard disc is usually designated as the **(C:)** drive.

Photographs, music and video files are very hungry for disc storage space. If you intend to use your computer in a big way for this type of storage, make sure you buy the biggest hard disc you can afford.

The Graphics Facilities

The quality of your screen display doesn't only depend on your chosen monitor, (the TV-like screen), though this is important. Electronic wizardry is needed to control the quality of the screen display and this may take two alternative forms; firstly *on-board* graphics components may be integrated into the *motherboard* i.e. the main circuit board inside of the computer.

Alternatively the graphics components may be supplied on a separate *graphics card*, as shown below. This is an example of an *expansion card*, a small printed circuit board which plugs into a spare slot in the motherboard.

For general use the standard graphics card supplied with most recent new computers should suffice. However, anyone doing a lot of high precision graphics work, etc., may need to fit a high quality graphics card. Some older machines may need to have a better graphics card fitted before they can run Windows Vista to its full potential. This means a graphics card with at least 128MB of its own memory on board, in addition to the RAM of the computer.

The Monitor

This is the screen on which you view your programs and Web pages. As mentioned earlier, the quality of the screen display depends not only on the monitor but also the specification of the graphics card or on-board graphics facilities. Monitor sizes are measured diagonally across the screen. 15-inch, 17-inch and 19-inch monitors are commonly used. Obviously large monitors are easier to read, especially if your eyesight is not what it used to be. I use the latest 19-inch flat screen TFT (*Thin-Film Transistor*) monitors costing about £110; these take up very little desk space compared with the earlier and much bulkier Cathode Ray Tube (CRT) monitors. An additional bonus is that some of these flat screen monitors have integral speakers, just visible on the bottom right and left of the monitor below; if you like music while you work these avoid the additional clutter of separate speakers.

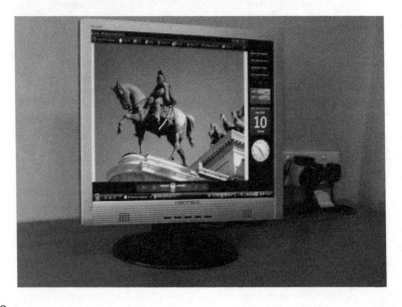

As discussed earlier, the quality of the screen display depends very much on the *graphics card* or on-board graphics components fitted to your computer. If you have difficulty reading the screen, Windows Vista has a built-in *Magnifier* feature which allows you to enlarge the text and graphics around the current cursor position on the screen. The magnifier is one of the **Ease of Access** features discussed later in this book in the chapter "Help for Users with Special Needs".

You can also adjust the screen *resolution* using the **Display Settings** feature in the **Personalize** section of the **Control Panel** (discussed shortly). The resolution is the number of small squares (known as *pixels* or *picture elements*) used to map out the screen. Typical screen resolutions are 800x600 and 1024x768. These are changed by using the mouse to drag a slider between **Low** and **High,** as shown below.

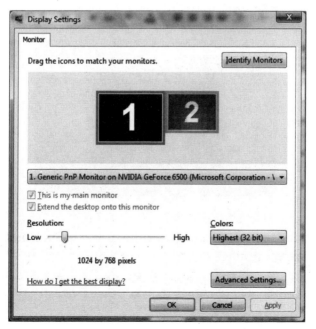

The Printer

A reliable printer is an essential part of your computer system – you can't do all of your communication by e-mail or posting on Web sites. A printer is needed to produce paper copies of letters, reports, accounts, publications, magazines, photographs, e-mails and Web pages.

Nowadays there are two popular types of printer used in the home and small business. These are the *laser printer* and the *inkjet*. You need to consider the type of work you will be doing in order to choose a suitable printer.

The Inkjet Printer

Inkjet printers are good all-rounders and can be bought for as little as £50, although models costing several hundred pounds are also available.

You must also consider the price of the black and colour ink cartridges which can cost from £10 – £20 or more per set. Inkjet printers can produce high quality colour photographs, though the cost of the cartridges and the special glossy paper makes this an expensive activity.

The Laser Printer

Laser printers are popular in the home and in business. They are fast, produce high quality printout and tend to be quieter than their main rival, the inkjet. Most laser printers are *mono* (i.e. they print only in black and white.) Mono laser printers suitable for the home or small business can be bought for less than £100, while colour laser printers cost from about £180 upwards. I have used two cheap mono laser printers over the last 10 years and they have been very reliable.

You need to shop around for replacement *toner cartridges* which typically cost around £40 – £50. *Toner* is a fine powder used as "ink" to print text and graphics. A toner cartridge should be capable of printing several thousand sheets of A4. *Refill toner kits* are a cheap way of extending the life of a cartridge although print quality may eventually suffer as the cartridge drum surface inevitably deteriorates.

Multi-purpose printers combine several functions such as printing, photocopying, sending faxes and scanning.

Internet Explorer 7, which is part of Windows Vista, has improved facilities for printing out copies of Web pages, compared with earlier versions of Internet Explorer.

Broadband Connections

Nowadays the traditional dial-up modem is considered too slow by many people, particularly for business use and for sending and receiving large files across the Internet. One answer to the need for more speed is the broadband system, introduced by BT and others. Home users of broadband have a service known as ADSL (Asymmetric Digital Subscriber Line). This converts a standard BT telephone line into a very fast Internet line. Comparing broadband to a normal modem line is like comparing a 6-lane motorway to a narrow country lane.

At the time of writing more than half of UK households have broadband and this is expected to increase to 4 out of 5 by the year 2010.

BT will check out the cable to your home and, if necessary, set up the actual connection. The line needs to be *activated* by BT before you can connect to the Internet.

To obtain a broadband connection, you will need to subscribe to a broadband Internet Service Provider such as BT Broadband, Tiscali or AOL. They will issue you with a *user name* and a *password*.

If you are already connected to the Internet with an ordinary modem and want to know more about broadband, the BT Web site (**http://www.bt.com/**) has details of prices and equipment needed, as shown on the right.

The Internet Service Provider should provide you with a pack containing everything you need.

The pack should contain:

- An instruction manual.
- A CD containing the set-up software.
- One or more *filters* and cables. A filter allows your computer and a telephone to be connected to a single phone line.
- Your username and password.
- Either an *ADSL modem* or a *wireless router*.

ADSL Modem

This is a small box which is connected by cables between the computer and the telephone line. Its purpose is to enable the computer, which uses digital data, to communicate over the telephone lines, which work with analogue (sound) data.

Wireless Router and Home Network

A wireless router allows several computers to share an Internet connection on a small home network, using radio signals. The router contains a built-in ADSL modem to connect to the Internet via a telephone line.  Every computer on the network must have a *wireless adaptor* fitted, in the form of a USB dongle or as an expansion card. The router is a fixed Internet *access point*. As the network is wireless you can set up your computer(s) in any room in your home. Or take a laptop computer down the garden and surf the net in the sunshine – wireless Internet works over quite large distances.

Summary of Broadband Features

Below is a list of the main features of a broadband Internet connection:

- Broadband is up to 100 times faster than an ordinary dial-up modem. So you can find and display information much faster and use *streaming* to view videos and TV programs online.

- You can send e-mails including pictures and video clips in *seconds* rather than *minutes*.

- You can download large files such as software, pictures and graphics from the Internet, in a fraction of the time taken by a dial-up modem. These are then saved on the hard disc of your computer.

- Once up and running in the morning, the computer stays *connected to the Internet all day*.

- You can use a single telephone line to make phone calls and "surf" the Internet *at the same time* – there's no need for a dedicated line.

- A monthly fee of about £20 – £30 includes unlimited access to the Internet. There are no call charges for using the Internet. The full cost including normal telephone line rental is about £50 – £60. There are also cut-price introductory offers for a limited period and at least one free broadband service where you pay only line rental.

Broadband is Desirable but not Essential

If you are on a limited income or don't need to download large files, etc., you can still enjoy using the Internet with a dial-up modem (admittedly at a more leisurely pace) – like most of us did quite happily before broadband arrived.

Hardware Requirements for Windows Vista

The development of new software always demands more and more powerful computers and Windows Vista is no exception. With its Aero 3D graphics and other facilities, Vista requires a computer with the sort of power unheard of amongst home users a few years ago. Most new computers should be capable of running Vista; indeed many new computers are supplied with Vista pre-installed.

However, if you are currently running a computer with an earlier version of Windows, such as Windows XP, as I was, you need to find answers to the following questions:

- Is the computer, in its present form, capable of running Windows Vista, including Windows Aero?

- If not, can the computer be upgraded with new components so that it's ready for Vista?

The next few pages explain how you can test your machine for Vista readiness.

Minimum Hardware Requirements for Vista Basic

Microsoft state that the <u>minimum</u> hardware requirements to run Vista are:

- A modern processor (at least 800MHz)

- 512MB of memory

- A graphics processor that is DirectX 9 capable.

Please note, these are minimum requirements – a machine which just meets this standard will not be able to run Windows Aero graphics, for example. (DirectX 9 above refers to software within Windows for displaying high quality graphics).

Hardware Needed to Run All Windows Vista Features

To get the full Windows Vista experience, including Windows Aero, Microsoft recommends a machine with the following specification or better:

- 1GHz processor
- 1GB of memory
- DirectX 9 graphics with 128MB of graphics memory on the graphics card
- 40GB of hard drive capacity with 15GB free
- DVD-ROM drive.

The term GHz above refers to the speed at which the processor can carry out instructions. Earlier, slower processors, operated at, say, 800 MHz or 800 million instructions per second. Nowadays, as processor speeds have increased, the M for Mega or millions has been replaced by G for Giga or thousands of millions.

Buying a New "Vista Ready" Computer

As an example, at the time of writing, one of the cheapest systems from a very large retailer, costing £350, has a 3.33GHz processor, 512MB memory, 160GB hard drive and integrated graphics. This should be able to run Vista Home Basic, but with only 512MB of memory it would not be able to run the Windows Aero graphics in the Vista Home Premium, Business and Ultimate versions. However, this computer could be upgraded easily and cheaply to run all Vista features by adding some more memory and fitting a new graphics card.

A more powerful machine, costing £500 from the same retailer, had a larger memory, superior graphics and should be able to run all of the Windows Vista features.

Checking an Existing Machine for Vista Readiness

If you are running an earlier version of Windows such as Windows XP, you can check your machine's main components by selecting **Start**, **Control Panel** and double-clicking the **System** icon (in **Classic View**). The **General** tab shown below reveals the specification of your computer.

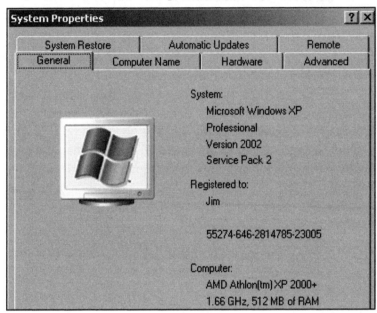

The above specification shows that this particular machine has an adequate **1.66GHz** processor; however, with only **512MB** of memory it will be limited to Vista Basic.

Clicking **Start** and **My Computer** in XP and pointing at the hard disc **(C:)** tells you the size of the hard disc and the free space. A 40GB hard disc with 15GB free is needed to run Vista at its highest level.

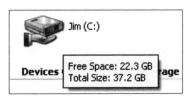

The Windows Vista Upgrade Advisor

You can carry out a thorough check to see if a computer is ready to run Windows Vista by downloading the **Upgrade Advisor**, a small piece of software from the Microsoft website at:

www.microsoft.com/windowsvista/getready/upgradeadvisor

The **Upgrade Advisor** examines your computer and produces a report listing any hardware or software upgrades needed to run Windows Vista. The sample report below states that a particular computer with "only" 512MB of memory (RAM) needs upgrading in order to run Windows Aero and other Vista features. Similarly the graphics card needs replacing and a Web link is provided to display a list of suitable cards. To fully display the Windows Aero 3D graphics a new graphics card must be compatible with DirectX 9 graphics technology and have at least 128MB of memory built onto the card itself.

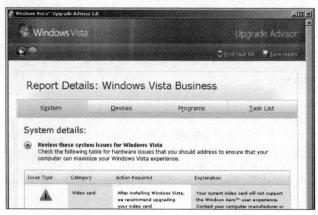

Upgrading a computer to run Vista is covered in detail in our companion book, Computing with Vista for the Older Generation, from Bernard Babani (publishing) Ltd.

Introducing
Windows Vista

What is Windows Vista?

After you switch the computer on, it starts up and in a short time the screen displays the Windows Vista Desktop with various icons and background scenery, as shown below.

During a session at the computer you would start programs like Microsoft Word or Internet Explorer by double-clicking the program's Desktop icon or selecting its name from the **Start/All Programs** menu. Then you might do an activity such as typing a letter, saving the letter on disc and printing it out on paper. All of these tasks are controlled by a collection of software known as the computer's *operating system*. Windows Vista is an operating system. To use your computer effectively you need to be familiar with the main components of Windows Vista outlined in this chapter.

Microsoft Windows, in various versions, has been the dominant operating system on personal computers for many years. Windows Vista is the latest version of Microsoft Windows and is installed as standard on many millions of new computers.

What Does Windows Vista Actually Do?

The Vista operating system provides the environment in which we control and interact with the computer. It presents the menus from which we select commands or tasks; it also controls the screen display and allows us to manage our document files and folders and to save and print our work. The operating system also controls peripheral devices such as scanners and modems and our connection to the Internet.

No matter what task we use our computer for, word processing, surfing the Internet, etc., the operating system will be working in the background in overall control.

Windows Vista also provides various tools for routine maintenance tasks and organizing your work. When you save a document, such as a letter, on your hard disc, the saved version is known as a *file*. A new **Instant Search** feature in Windows Vista enables you to quickly find files stored anywhere on your computer. The Windows operating system allows you to arrange your files into a system of organized folders. Windows is also used for deleting any files of work which you no longer need.

Windows Vista includes its own *applications* software such as Internet Explorer 7. This is a *Web browser*, a program used for searching the Internet and displaying information, such as bargain holidays or herbal remedies. Internet Explorer 7 is discussed in detail later in this book.

Windows Vista Built-in Applications

Windows Vista includes many applications, i.e. pieces of software for performing specific tasks. These can be found in the **Start/All Programs** menu and in the **Accessories** sub-menu of the **All Programs** menu. For example, **WordPad** is a basic but capable word processor shown on the right.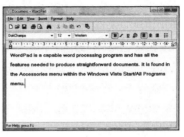

Windows Paint is a drawing and painting program. It can also be used for, amongst other things, cropping photos and saving files in different formats. These include the popular JPEG format used for sending picture files over the Internet.

The **Windows Media Player** shown on the right turns your computer into an impressive entertainment centre, with easily managed personal libraries of music and video clips. CDs can be copied to your hard disc and music can be "burned" from your hard disc to a new CD.

The **Windows Media Center** enables your computer to be turned into a television, allowing you to watch live programs and record them on DVD. A *TV tuner* (expansion card or USB dongle) must be fitted to your computer.

The Evolution of Microsoft Windows Vista

Windows Vista is the latest in a line of Microsoft Windows operating systems, starting with Windows 3.0 and Windows 3.1, followed by Windows 95, Windows 98 and Windows Me. Business users were provided with separate versions of Windows, namely Windows NT and Windows 2000. Windows XP arrived in 2001 and was the result of a merger between the Windows home and business versions.

Windows has been under constant development since the introduction of Windows XP, initially having the working title of Windows Longthorn and culminating in Windows Vista, first available to the general public in early 2007.

Windows Vista introduces many spectacular new features and these are discussed shortly.

Versions of Windows Vista

There are four versions of Vista – Home Basic, Home Premium, Business and Ultimate; your choice of version depends on the way you use your computer and how much you are prepared to pay. For example, Home Basic will suffice if you want to do general tasks such as office work – word processing, spreadsheets, Internet and e-mail, etc. Vista Home Basic lacks some entertainment features such as Windows Media Center and also the stunning new 3D graphics effects known as Windows Aero, discussed shortly. Home Premium includes Windows Aero and also the Windows Media Center. The Business version of Vista includes Windows Aero and has additional networking and backup features. To get the best of all worlds, Windows Vista Ultimate incorporates all of the new Vista features, including Windows Aero together with the entertainment, backup, data protection and networking facilities.

A Brief Tour of Windows Vista

Many of the features in earlier versions of Windows are still present in Vista, though they may have changed and been improved. There are also many new features in Windows Vista such as Windows Aero – stunning graphics which are both easy to use and pleasing to the eye.

The next few pages describe some of the main features of Windows Vista, particularly those which should appeal to mature readers for whom this book is primarily intended. Many of the new Vista features are covered in more detail in later chapters in this book. For example, the **Ease of Use** facilities and **Speech Recognition** are covered in the chapter "Help for Users with Special Needs". **Ease of Use** replaces the **Accessibility** features found in Windows XP.

Launching Windows Vista

Windows Vista includes a new **Start** icon or *orb*, replacing the **Start** button in earlier versions of Windows. Clicking **Start** leads to a redesigned **Start** menu with your frequently used programs in the left-hand panel, as shown on the next page. In the right-hand panel there are links to many of the most useful Windows Vista features such as the **Control Panel** and **Computer** (formerly known as **My Computer** in earlier versions of Windows). The **Control Panel** is an important tool used for setting up hardware and software. **Computer** displays the resources such as hard discs, CD drives and removable flash drives attached to your computer. The **Control Panel** and **Computer** are discussed in more detail in the next chapter.

Also shown in the right-hand pane above is a link to **Recent Items**. This allows you to return instantly to documents you have been working on recently, such as Word documents you have created or photographs you've been editing.

Internet Explorer 7

Windows Vista contains a lot of built-in software. This includes Internet Explorer, a program known as a *Web browser* which is used to find and display pages on the Internet. Web pages can be saved on your hard disc, printed on paper or "bookmarked" for future reference.

Most Web pages contain several *links* (also known as *hyperlinks*). These are pieces of text, icons or pictures which you click to open up another Web page or Web site which may be on another computer anywhere in the world.

Windows Vista includes Internet Explorer version 7, which is also available for users of Windows XP, the forerunner to Windows Vista. Internet Explorer 7 introduces many new features which have been widely welcomed. These include *tabbed browsing* which allows you to move easily between several Web pages open simultaneously. Internet Explorer 7 and Web pages are discussed in more detail in the remainder of this book.

The Instant Search Feature

From time to time most of us probably forget the folders or locations on the hard disc where we saved files. The **Instant Search** feature in Windows Vista rapidly finds items saved anywhere on your hard disc. Simply type the name (or just part of the name) of the file into the **Start Search** bar at the bottom of the **Start** menu shown on the previous page. For example, I knew I had saved a photograph as a file called **cats**; the name of the file is entered into the **Start Search** bar shown below and on the previous page.

In no time at all, the file is found and displayed in the **Search Results** window shown in the extract below.

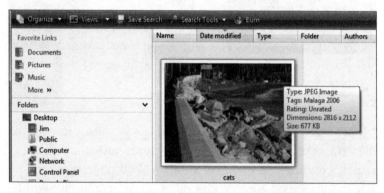

Passing the mouse cursor over the icon for the file reveals the file details, as shown in the small rectangle on the right above. Double-clicking the **cats** icon (shown in extra large view above) opens up the file in its associated program. In this example, as **cats** is a photograph, the file is opened in Adobe Photoshop Elements, the photo editing program on this computer. In the same way a word processing document would open in Microsoft Word or similar.

Windows Aero

This is a brand-new feature introduced with Windows Vista and dramatically changes the way we see and interact with items on the screen – the "graphical user interface". To receive Windows Aero in all its glory, you need a computer equipped with quite high quality graphics facilities. If your machine is lacking in either hardware or software, you may still be able to run Vista Basic but may miss out on the more spectacular 3D effects of Windows Aero.

The section on hardware requirements which follows later in this book shows how you can run a test on your computer for compatibility with Windows Vista.

Live Taskbar Thumbnails

If you are running several programs on your computer at a given time, recent versions of Windows display an icon for each program and details of the file and program on the Taskbar on the bottom of the screen. However, in Windows Aero, passing the cursor over the item on the Taskbar also displays a large thumbnail, giving a clear view of the contents of the file, as shown on the lower right below.

Windows Flip

While working away at the computer you may have a lot of windows open but with only one window maximized on the screen at a given time. For example when producing a document such as a chapter in this book, I often have more than one word processing document and various **Paint** images open in their own windows but running invisibly in the background. You may want to switch from one window to another, but may be unsure what each window contains. Windows Flip displays live thumbnails as shown below. This enables you to quickly identify and select the window

 you want. Simply hold down the **Alt** key and repeatedly press the **Tab** key (shown left) to move through and highlight each thumbnail.

When the window you want to use is highlighted, release the **Alt** key to maximise the window.

Examples of thumbnails representing a variety of running programs are shown above. Reading from left to right, these are, in this particular example:

- A photograph in Windows Paint.
- A chapter of this book running in Microsoft Word.
- The Windows Vista Computer feature.
- The Windows Vista Desktop.

Windows Flip 3D

This is probably the most spectacular of the Aero features; like Windows Flip it's very useful when you've a lot of windows open and need to switch between them. For example, you might want return to the Desktop and then start a program such as Internet Explorer by double-clicking its icon. To launch Flip 3D, hold down the **Windows** key, marked with the Windows logo and perhaps the word **Start**, as shown on the right.

A press of the **Tab** key displays all of your currently open windows in 3D on the screen, as shown below.

Repeatedly pressing the **Tab** key, (or turning the scroll wheel on the mouse) while holding down the **Windows** key, rotates the windows on the screen as if on a carousel. As each window is brought to the front, you can open it, maximized on the screen, by simply releasing the **Windows** key. Clicking any of the windows in the Flip 3D stack shown above, while the **Windows** key is still held down, maximises that window on the screen.

The Windows Vista Sidebar

The Sidebar in Windows Vista is a pane, normally down the right-hand side of the screen, which displays small programs or mini-applications, such as a clock, the weather, or news flashes (also known as *RSS feeds*, discussed later). The sidebar items appear in small individual windows, as shown on the right below, and are known as **gadgets**.

The Sidebar above on the right shows at the top a gadget displaying news headlines, then below it a slideshow of photographs, which can be selected from your own folders. Next there is a notepad into which you can type any text you like, such as reminders, followed by a clock at the bottom. Clicking the small plus sign (shown on the right) at the top of the Sidebar presents the **Gadgets Gallery**, as shown on the next page.

Gadgets are added to the Sidebar by double-clicking their thumbnail in the Gadget Gallery as shown above. Further gadgets can be obtained by clicking the Internet link, **Get more gadgets online** at the bottom right of the Gallery.

If you right-click over a gadget, a menu appears with options to **Close Gadget** or **Detach from Sidebar**, for example; when a gadget such as a clock is detached it can be dragged and placed anywhere on the screen.

Right-clicking over the Sidebar itself and then clicking **Properties** presents a dialogue box with options to display the Sidebar when Windows starts up, to place it on the left or right of the screen, and to always show the Sidebar on top of other windows. The Windows Sidebar icon on the right of the Taskbar at the bottom of the screen can be used to display the Sidebar; when the icon is right-clicked a menu appears, including options to change the **Properties** or **Exit** the sidebar.

The Windows Photo Gallery

This is a new feature introduced with Windows Vista and enables you to display and manage your photographs and videos easily. The Windows **Photo Gallery** can be opened from the **Start** menu or the **Start/All Programs** menu.

The menu across the top of the **Photo Gallery** is shown below and includes a drop-down **File** menu with an option **Add Folder to Gallery...**, to copy existing photos on your hard disc to the gallery. Alternatively you can import pictures directly from a digital camera or scanner.

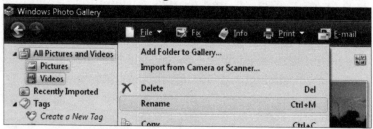

The **Photo Gallery** in Windows Vista contains its own tools for enhancing photographs selected in the gallery. These tools are shown on the left and are accessed by clicking **Fix** on the menu bar shown on the previous page. **Crop Picture** allows you to cut away unwanted areas of the photo. **Fix Red Eye** corrects an unwanted phenomenon which occurs in photos of people and animals.

The **Print** option shown on the **Photo Gallery** menu bar enables you to specify the type of paper and the finished size of your prints. Further options allow you to send your photos as e-mail attachments or "burn" images to a CD.

Tags

Tags are used to organize photographs and any other type of file. A large number of photographs can be labelled with tags representing various smaller categories. Suppose you have perhaps 100 photos in your **Photo Gallery** and you want to extract just the images of garden birds, for

example. First you create a new tag, **Garden Birds**. Then all the images of garden birds are selected and dragged from the **Photo Gallery** and dropped over the new tag. In future, to look at just garden birds you would click the **Garden Birds** tag. The

images remain in the main pool of the **Photo Gallery** but the tags allow certain groups to be extracted very quickly.

Good Housekeeping Tools in Windows Vista
The System Tools Menu

Windows Vista contains a number of tools for keeping your computer running at its optimum performance. Several of these are to be found in the **System Tools** menu opened by selecting **Start**, **All Programs**, **Accessories** and **System Tools**, as shown below.

Disk Cleanup shown above should be used regularly to remove temporary and redundant files.

Disk Fragmenter helps your computer to run faster and more efficiently by optimizing the way files are stored on the hard disc. Vista schedules this tool automatically but you can also run it manually from the **System Tools** menu.

System Restore can be used if a problem develops, perhaps after installing new software. **System Restore** returns the system to a previously good configuration or **Restore Point**. You can create and save your own **Restore Points**.

System Information displays the specification of some of the main components of your computer.

The Recycle Bin

Files and folders can be deleted by selecting the file in the window of the **Computer** feature in Windows Vista, then pressing the **Delete** key. In fact this does not wipe the file or folder from your hard disc but merely removes it to a location called the **Recycle Bin**. This can be opened by double-clicking its icon on the Windows Vista Desktop as shown on the left. Files in the recycle bin can still be restored to their original location. You can click a button to **Wipe the Recycle Bin** to permanently remove files from your hard disc. The **Disk Cleanup** feature mentioned on the previous page also empties the **Recycle Bin**.

Windows Update

This feature connects your computer to the Internet and checks for any new Windows software which you may wish to download from the Internet to your computer. Updates are usually utility files which improve the security or enhance the performance of your computer. You can run **Windows Update** from **Start** and **All Programs**. In the **Control Panel** in **Classic View** double-click the **Windows Update** icon shown on the left. In **Control Panel Home** select **System and Maintenance** to display the following options.

If you click **Turn automatic updating on or off** as shown above, you can schedule a daily automatic update of your Windows software; alternatively you can view the updates on offer and decide if you want to install them.

A Closer Look into Windows Vista

This chapter looks at the feature in Vista known simply as Computer. The Computer feature, together with the Windows Explorer, is used for viewing and organising your computer's discs and your files and folders; the Control Panel, discussed shortly, is used for setting up hardware devices like printers and installing and removing software such as a word processing program. This chapter also has a closer look at the make-up of on-screen windows and the use of the mouse to work with screen objects such as menus and dialogue boxes.

The Computer Feature

Click the **Start** orb or button at the bottom left-hand side of the screen and then click **Computer** from the right-hand side of the **Start** menu which appears.

The **Computer** feature opens in its own window as shown below. You can see that on this particular computer there is a floppy disc drive **A:**, a hard disc drive **C:** , a DVD drive **E:** and a removable disc **G:** Information is given about each disc drive, such as the amount of free space, measured in gigabytes (GB), as discussed on page 25.

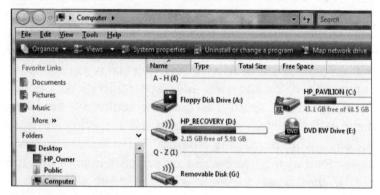

The Windows Explorer

The Windows Explorer is used for displaying the resources on your computer, such as hard discs and folders, etc. A quick way to start the Windows Explorer is by right-clicking the **Start** orb and selecting **Explore** from the menu (shown on the right) which pops up. You can also select **Windows Explorer** from the **Accessories** menu in **Start/All Programs**. The windows opened in the Windows Explorer and in the Computer feature will be referred to from now on as Explorer windows.

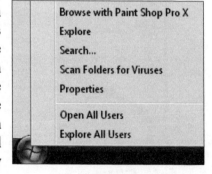

To reveal the contents of any of the discs, such as the hard disc **C:**, double-click its entry in the **Explorer** window. Very quickly a full listing of all the folders on drive **C:** appears as shown below.

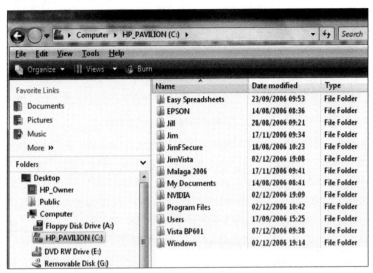

To view the files contained in any of the folders, double-click anywhere on the folder name or icon. For example, double-clicking the folder **Jim** above produced the following.

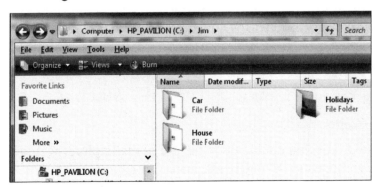

Double-clicking the **Car** folder shown on the previous page reveals that it contains a Word document, **Accident Report**, shown below.

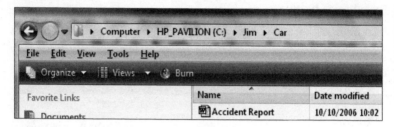

Opening a File in its Associated Program

Double-clicking anywhere on the name or icon for the file **Accident Report** shown above opens the file in its *associated program*, in this case Microsoft Word. The associated program is normally the program used to create a file; however you can set a file to be opened in another program on your computer, if it's compatible with the file.

For example, an image or photographic file might be set to open in any one of several available photo editing programs, such as Paint Shop Pro or Adobe Photoshop, etc.

To associate a program with a file type, right-click over the file's name in the Explorer window. Then select the program's name in the **Open With** sub-menu which appears, as shown below. This is now the associated program.

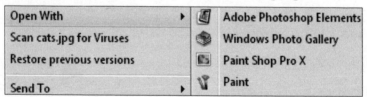

Next time you double-click the file in the Explorer window it will open in the newly associated program.

Displaying Folders in Windows Vista

Windows Vista introduces attractive and helpful ways of displaying files and folders using **Live Icons** in Explorer windows, making it easier to find items such as documents and photos, etc. Stored files and folders can be viewed by selecting **Start**, **Computer**, then double-clicking over the hard disc drive, usually **C:**, as shown below.

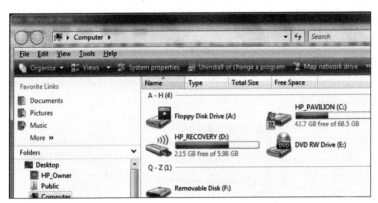

Similarly you could double-click the icon for the CD drive **E:** or the removable disc **F:** as shown in the above example.

With **View** and **Large Icons** selected from the Explorer menu bar, Vista displays the folders in 3D, revealing the type of documents saved within each folder, as shown below.

Malaga 2006   My Documents   NVIDIA

Displaying Files in Windows Vista

In Windows Vista the **Live Icons** feature presents a miniature image of a document in the Explorer window, rather than just a small icon for the file type. The images show you what a file actually contains, without you having to open the file in the appropriate program, such as a word processor, spreadsheet or photo editor, for example. Two images representing photo files are shown below in the Vista Explorer window.

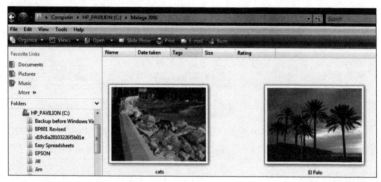

The **Views** menu in Windows Vista allows your files to be displayed in the Explorer window in several different ways.

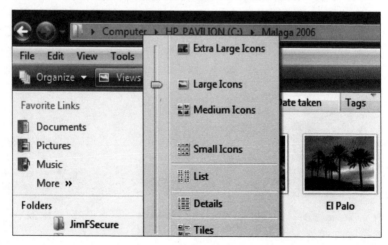

As can be seen on the menu at bottom of the previous page, there are many different ways of viewing files and folders in the Vista Explorer window. For example, **Extra Large Icons** displays the sort of image shown on the left, while the **Details** view shown below gives specific information, such as the date and time the file or folder was created.

Malaga 2006	17/11/2006 09:41	File Folder

Searching in the Explorer Window

The Explorer windows used for displaying and copying files and folders now include a new **Instant Search** bar. To start **Explorer**, right-click over the **Start** orb at the bottom left of the screen and select **Explore** from the pop-up menu.

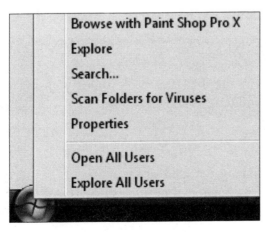

The Explorer window opens as shown below. The left-hand pane shows all of your resources such as the hard disc **C:** and any removable discs such as flash drives, etc. If you select the **C:** drive, all of your folders are displayed in the right-hand pane shown below.

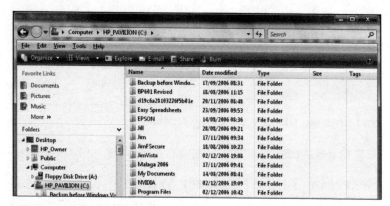

At the top right of the Explorer window is a **Search** bar, as shown above. You can enter here the name of any file or folder on your hard disc and Vista will quickly find it. For example, I entered **El Palo**, the name of a photographic file, as shown below.

A listing of the file was very quickly displayed in the Explorer window, as shown below.

Name	Date modified	Type	Folder
El Palo	01/01/2004 00:00	JPG File	Malaga 2006 (C:)

Double-clicking the icon or the name of the file opens the file in its associated program, such as Adobe Photoshop Elements, for example.

The Control Panel

This is a very important feature used for making alterations to the hardware and software on your computer. For example, the Control Panel can be used to install or remove software and to alter settings such as the screen resolution, the screen saver and the colours used to display windows. The Control Panel is started by clicking the **Start** button and then selecting **Control Panel** from the right of the **Start** menu, as shown in the extract below.

The Control Panel opens up in its own window in one of the following two views, **Control Panel Home** and **Classic View**, as shown on the next two pages. **Control Panel Home** groups the various tasks into categories under relevant headings. A single click of a heading or icon in **Control Panel Home** displays further options.

Classic View presents a large number of icons representing many different tasks. To start a task in **Classic View** you double-click the appropriate icon.

You can switch between **Control Panel Home** and **Classic View** by clicking the appropriate view at the top left of the **Control Panel** Window, as shown on the left.

Control Panel Home

As shown below, **Control Panel Home** uses descriptive text to provide links to various tasks.

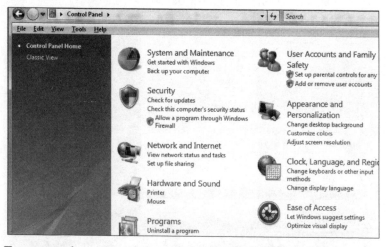

For example, **Appearance and Personalization** above allows you to adjust screen settings, colours and resolution. **Ease of Access** presents a number of features designed to help people with special needs, as discussed in the next chapter. **Programs** allows you to uninstall software, while **User Accounts and Family Safety** enables, amongst other things, parents (and grandparents) to limit the time children spend on the Internet. You can also control the programs and Web pages which children can access. **Hardware and Sound** enables you to adjust settings on devices such as printers, mice and your sound system.

The Control Panel in Classic View

Double-clicking an icon in the **Control Panel** in **Classic View** shown below takes you directly to a specific task.

For example, double-clicking the **Mouse** icon allows you to adjust the speed and functions of the mouse buttons and the mouse scroll wheel; also the way the mouse pointer appears and behaves.

Mouse

To find out the status of your printer and to solve printing problems, double-click the **Printers** icon. This feature allows you to delete print jobs, set a printer as default and clean inkjet printer heads, for example.

Printers

The search bar at the top right of the **Control Panel** window in both **Classic** and **Home** views allows you to type in the name or even just the first few letters of a tool; then the icon for the tool appears instantly. For example, entering **fir** displays the **Windows Firewall** icon. Switching the **Firewall** on is intended to protect your computer from hackers, etc.

Windows Firewall

Working with Windows

Windows are rectangular boxes on the screen, used to frame the current task. A window might contain, for example:

- A document in an *application* such as a word processor, drawing program or a spreadsheet.

- A display, in the Vista Computer feature, of the discs, etc., connected to your machine.

- A listing in the Windows Explorer of the hierarchy of folders stored on your hard disc, etc.

- The set of icons or a list of tasks in the Control Panel, used for setting up hardware and software.

Although windows are used for such diverse purposes, in general they contain the same basic components. Shortly we will look at the make-up of a typical window. However, since the mouse plays a central role in the operation of windows, let's look at the use of the mouse in some detail.

You can tailor the mouse and pointer to work in various ways. Select **Start**, **Control Panel** and make sure **Classic View** is selected. Double-click the mouse icon, shown on the right, to make various adjustments to the way the mouse and pointer work. These include swapping the functions of the left-hand and right-hand buttons and also altering the double-click speed. You can also vary the amount of vertical and horizontal scrolling caused by the movement of the *scroll wheel* located in the centre of the mouse, between the left-hand and right-hand buttons.

Mouse Operations

Click

This means a single press of the left-hand mouse button. With the cursor over an icon or screen object, a click will cause, for example, a command from a menu to be carried out or a folder to open.

Double Click

This means pressing the left mouse button very quickly twice in succession. This is often used to carry out operations such as starting a program from an icon on the Windows Desktop. Folders can be set to open with either a single or double click.

Right Click

Pressing the right button while the pointer is over a screen object is a quick way to open up additional menus relating to the object. For example, if you right-click over the **Start** button on the Vista Taskbar, a menu appears giving, amongst other things, a quick way to start the Windows Explorer.

Open

Browse with Paint Shop Pro X

Explore

Search...

Scan Folders for Viruses

Properties

Dragging and Dropping

This is used to move objects about the screen, such as moving files and folders into different folders. Click over the object, then, keeping the left-hand button held down, move the mouse pointer (together with the object) to the new position. Release the left button to place the object in its new position. Dragging is also used to resize windows and graphics on the screen and for *selecting* or *highlighting* a piece of text to be edited.

The Parts of a Window

The window below shows the major features common to most **Explorer** windows.

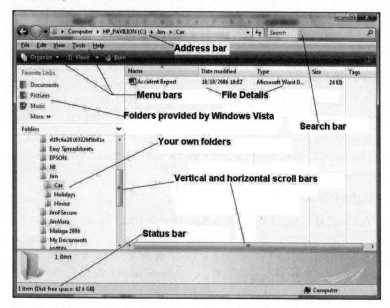

Along the top of the Explorer window shown above are **Forward** and **Back** arrow buttons, also displayed on the left below. These allow you to navigate between files and folders that have been viewed previously.

Folders in Vista can be arranged in a tree structure and may contain other folders, known as *sub-folders*, as well as files or documents. This is illustrated by the **Address Bar** shown below; this displays the *path* through the folders to the currently selected folder, **Car**.

> ▶ Computer ▶ HP_PAVILION (C:) ▶ Jim ▶ Car

The Instant Search Bar

On the right of the Explorer window is the **Instant Search** bar. Type any word or part  of a word into the search bar and if a file or folder of that name exists anywhere on your system it will be quickly found. Then it can be opened in its associated program by double-clicking its name or icon, as discussed earlier.

Maximising and Minimising, etc.

As shown on the previous pages, the Vista windows have three heavily used buttons in the top right-hand corner.

The Minimise Button

This reduces a window to a small item on the Taskbar at the bottom of the screen, as shown below. Click a Taskbar item to restore a minimized window to its original size.

The Maximise Button

This expands a window to fill the whole screen.

The Restore Button

After a window has been maximized, the middle icon changes to the Restore icon shown on the right. This returns the window to its previous size.

The Close Button

This window stops any program that is currently running and closes the window. You will be given the chance to save any unsaved work.

Resizing a Window or Pane

The main window and the rectangular panes within it can be expanded or contracted by dragging a small double arrow (◂▸) which appears when the cursor is allowed to dwell on a vertical or horizontal border line or a corner.

Scroll Bars and Scroll Buttons

Horizontal and vertical scroll bars and buttons allow you to pan a large image which is too big to fit inside a window.

Menu Bars in Explorer Windows

Near the top left of the **Explorer** window shown earlier is the Menu Bar. This appears on a lot of windows and usually starts with **File**, **Edit** and **View**, etc.

File   Edit   View   Tools   Help

Clicking any of these causes a drop-down menu to appear, with options to perform common tasks. For example the **Edit** menu has options to **Cut** (i.e. delete), **Copy** or **Paste** a selected file or folder.

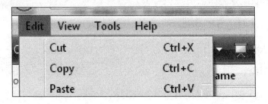

The previous **Edit** menu might be used to move a file or folder from location to another. This can also be done by dragging and dropping a file or folder with the mouse.

Clicking **View** as shown above presents a drop-down menu which includes options to alter the size of the icons used to represent files and folders in the Explorer window.

You can also choose to show details of the files, such as their size and when they were created as discussed earlier.

A second menu bar has a row of menus which expands and contracts depending on the item selected in the right-hand pane in the **Explorer** window. This menu starts with **Organize**, **Views** and **Burn** as shown below.

Some of the menu options under **Organize**, **Views**, etc., are the same as options on the **File**, **Edit**, **View**, etc., menu.

When an object is selected in the right-hand panel of the Explorer Window shown earlier, extra menus and options may appear on the lower menu

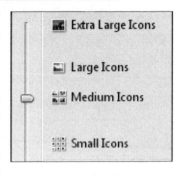

bar, as shown below. These might include, for example, **Open**, **Print**, **E-mail** and **Burn** (copy to a CD).

If, say, photographic files are selected in the Explorer window, a **Slide Show** icon appears on the menu bar, as shown below.

Dialogue Boxes

The windows just discussed contain running programs and folders, whereas *dialogue boxes* (as shown below) usually require the user to enter information or specify settings. (Windows Vista provides *default* settings and names which will suffice until you are ready to insert your own settings.)

Dialogue boxes appear after you select a menu command which ends in an ellipsis (...) such as **Save As**... and **Print...**. The **Print** dialogue box shown below contains many of the features common to dialogue boxes.

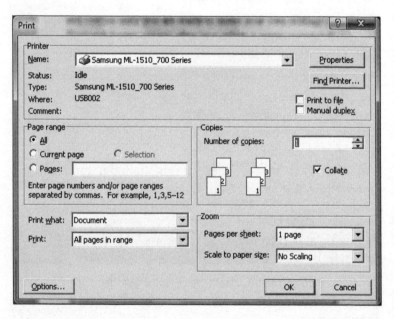

The white circles under **Page range** on the previous dialogue box are known as *radio buttons*, switched on or off with a single click. Only one radio button in a group can be selected at a given time.

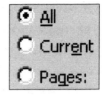

The white squares next to **Print to file**, **Manual duplex** and **Collate** are known as *check boxes*. Any number of check boxes can be switched on, i.e. ticked, at a given time.

Clicking the *down arrow* on the right of a horizontal bar reveals a *drop-down menu* of choices, such as several printers, as shown below.

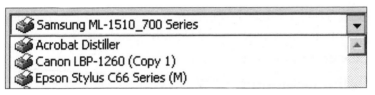

Some dialogue boxes have a *text bar* which allows you to type in your own words, such as a file or folder name. For example, when you select **Save As...** from the **File** menu, the **Save As...** dialogue box appears. This includes an icon to create a new folder, shown on the right. Click this icon and then enter a name for the new folder in the text box which appears, as shown below. Then click **OK** to create the new folder.

Creating Shortcut Icons on the Vista Desktop

Shortcuts to Programs

To provide a shortcut icon on the Vista Desktop for any of your programs, first select **All Programs** from the **Start** menu. Next right-click the name or icon for the program and click **Send To**. Now select **Desktop (create shortcut)** to place an icon on the Windows Vista Desktop.

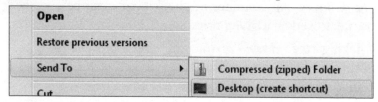

From now on the program can be started by double-clicking the new icon on the Desktop, as shown below.

Shortcuts to Files and Folders

Right-click the name of the file or folder in the Windows Explorer. From the pop-up menu use **Send To** and **Desktop (create shortcut)** as before. Double-click the new icon on the Vista Desktop to open the file or folder.

As shown in the extract from my own desktop below, there is a shortcut icon, **Vista BP601**, to a folder containing the text of one of our other books. Also shown are icons for frequently-used programs such as **Adobe Photoshop Elements**, the **Google** Internet search engine, the Windows **Paint** program and **Internet Explorer**, the component of Windows Vista used for "surfing" the Internet.

Help for Users with Special Needs

Windows Vista contains a number of **Ease of Access** features designed to help common impairments, affecting faculties such as, for example:

- Eyesight
- Dexterity
- Hearing
- Speech

Some users with greater needs may require more specialised accessibility software and equipment than the tools available in Windows Vista. As discussed shortly, further help can be found by entering keywords into an Internet search "engine" (i.e. program) such as Google.

The **Ease of Access** menu is launched by selecting **Start**, **All Programs**, **Accessories** and **Ease of Access**. (You may need to scroll down the list of programs 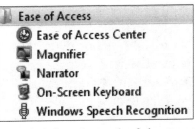 in the **All Programs** menu in the left-hand panel of the **Start** menu until **Accessories** is visible.)

The next section looks at the five **Ease of Access** features, shown in the menu on the right above.

The Ease of Access Center

This feature can be launched in several ways. For example, click **Start**, **Control Panel** and double-click the icon shown on the right in the **Control Panel** in **Classic View**. Alternatively you can open the **Ease of Access Center** from **Control Panel Home** as shown below:

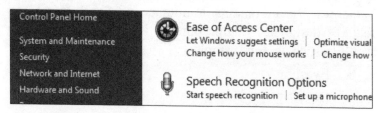

Next select **Ease of Access Center**, as shown above, to see the full list of accessibility tools.

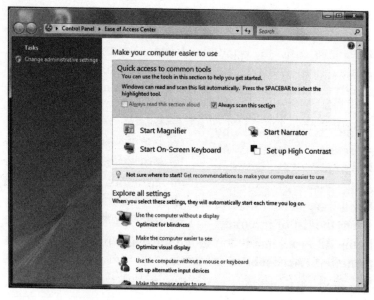

The Magnifier

As shown in the previous window, you can go directly to any of the various **Ease of Access** tools, such as the **Magnifier**, for example. The **Magnifier** produces an enlarged display of the text and graphics around the current cursor position.

The Narrator

The **Narrator** reads out aloud the contents of the windows displayed on the screen, including titles, menu options, features such as buttons and check boxes, and keys as they are typed.

The On-Screen Keyboard

If you find a normal keyboard difficult to use, you can "type" by using the mouse to click the letters on the image of a keyboard on the screen.

High Contrast

This option makes the screen easier to read by increasing the contrast on colours.

The above features are discussed in more detail shortly.

Finding Out Your Own Special Needs

If you are not sure which tools you need to help you, the **Ease of Access Center** allows you to select your particular needs from several lists of impairments. Then a list of recommended settings is produced which you may choose to switch on if you wish. To start entering your own difficulties, click on **Get recommendations to make your computer easier to use**, halfway down the **Ease of Access Center** window, as shown below and on the previous page.

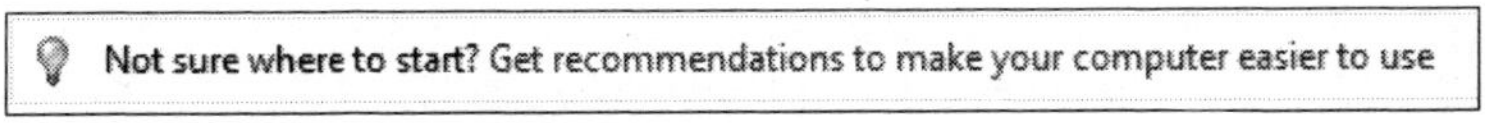

> 💡 Not sure where to start? Get recommendations to make your computer easier to use

You are presented with a series of statements under the headings **Eyesight**, **Dexterity**, **Hearing**, **Speech** and **Reasoning**. Each statement is preceded by a check box, which you can tick by clicking with the mouse if it applies to you. For example, the **Eyesight** statements are shown below:

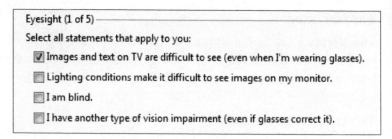

After you click **Next**, the investigation of your needs continues with the statements on **Dexterity**, **Hearing**, **Speech** and **Reasoning**. Finally you are presented with a list of recommended settings which you may choose to switch on by clicking to tick the check box, as shown below:

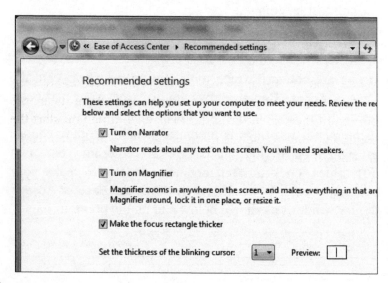

The list of **Recommended settings** shown previously may also include options to change the colour and size of the mouse pointers:

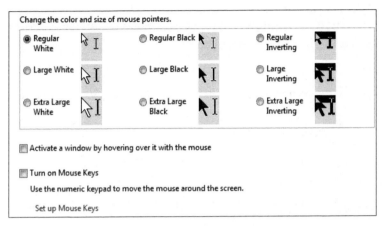

Other options include **Turn on Sticky Keys**. Some keyboard "shortcuts" require three keys on the keyboard to be pressed simultaneously. **Sticky Keys** allow these operations to be reduced to a single key press.

Turn on Mouse Keys shown above enables the numeric keypad (on the right of the keyboard) and also the arrow keys, to move the mouse pointer around the screen.

When you've finished selecting your **Ease of Access** recommended settings, click **Apply** and **Save** near the bottom of the screen. From now on, each time you start the computer, your chosen features, such as the **Magnifier** or the **On-Screen Keyboard**, will start up automatically.

At the bottom of the list of **Ease of Access** recommendations is a clickable link to a Web site giving further information about organisations and products intended to make computers easier to use.

Learn about additional assistive technologies online

You can also access the various **Ease of Access** settings directly rather than by completing the list of statements relating to **Eyesight**, **Dexterity**, **Hearing**, **Speech** and **Reasoning**, discussed earlier in this chapter. The settings are listed in the lower part of the **Ease of Access Center** under the heading **Explore all settings**.

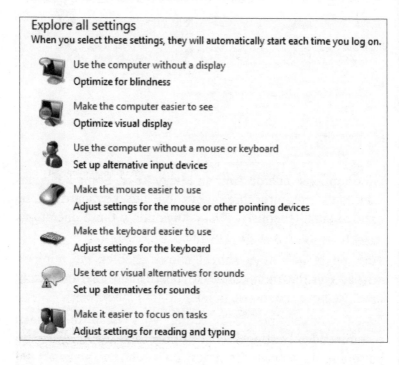

Explore all settings
When you select these settings, they will automatically start each time you log on.

Use the computer without a display
Optimize for blindness

Make the computer easier to see
Optimize visual display

Use the computer without a mouse or keyboard
Set up alternative input devices

Make the mouse easier to use
Adjust settings for the mouse or other pointing devices

Make the keyboard easier to use
Adjust settings for the keyboard

Use text or visual alternatives for sounds
Set up alternatives for sounds

Make it easier to focus on tasks
Adjust settings for reading and typing

For example, **Use the computer without a mouse or keyboard** enables you to set up alternative input devices, such as the **On-Screen Keyboard** or to control the computer using a microphone and **Speech Recognition** (discussed shortly).

The Magnifier

If you are finding the text and graphics difficult to read, you can enlarge the area around the current cursor position by switching on the **Magnifier** in the **Ease of Access Center**.

Select **Start**, **Control Panel** and **Ease of Access**. Then click **Start Magnifier** in the **Ease of Access Center** shown below.

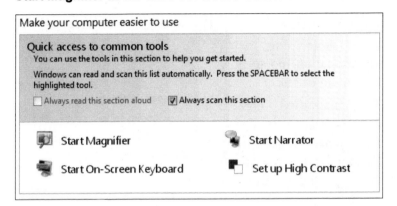

The magnified text and graphics appear in a separate window at the top of the screen, as shown below.

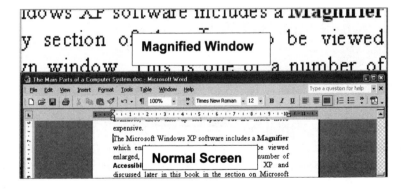

The **Magnifier** also appears as a minimised icon on the Windows Vista Taskbar as shown below.

If you click this icon, the **Magnifier** window opens, presenting a number of settings which can be adjusted. These include the **Scale factor** for the magnification, up to a maximum of **16x**.

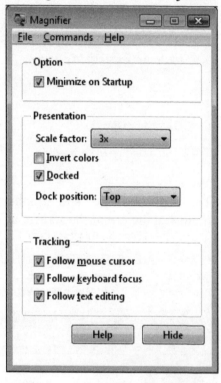

The magnified area can be placed at the **Top**, **Left**, **Right** or **Bottom** of the screen, using the **Dock position** option shown on the right. The **Magnifier** dialogue box window shown on the right can be set to start up either minimised or full size.

The **Magnifier** can be switched off by clicking the **Close** icon in the top right-hand corner of the window. Alternatively, right-click over the **Magnifier** Taskbar icon and click **Close** off the menu which pops up.

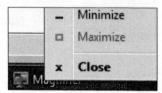

The On-Screen Keyboard

Click **Start On-Screen Keyboard** in the **Ease of Access Center** shown on page 83. The keyboard image immediately pops up on the screen, as shown below:

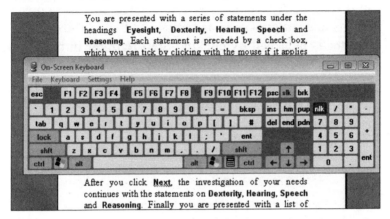

There is also an icon for the **On-Screen Keyboard** on the Vista Taskbar at the bottom of the screen.

Place the cursor where you want to begin typing and simply point to and click the required letters and characters. Upper or lower case letters are obtained by clicking one of the on-screen **shft** keys. The **On-Screen Keyboard** can be moved to a convenient position by dragging in the Title Bar to the right of the words **On-Screen Keyboard**.

To switch off the **On-Screen Keyboard**, click the **Close** icon in the top right-hand corner of the keyboard or right-click the Taskbar icon and click the **Close** option on the menu which pops up.

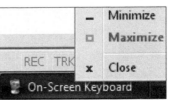

The Narrator

If your computer has the sound facility set up, you can use the **Narrator** to give a spoken commentary as you work. The **Narrator** tells you what keys you've pressed and also reads out details of any windows you've opened, including menu options and features such as buttons and check boxes. The **Narrator** is launched by clicking **Start Narrator** in the **Ease of Access Center**, as shown on page 83.

After a few seconds the **Narrator** window appears, allowing you to make various adjustments to the settings. There is also a **Microsoft Narrator** icon on the Vista Taskbar.

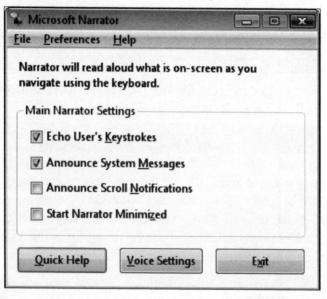

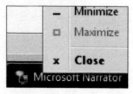 The **Narrator** can be closed by clicking **Exit** or the **Close** button shown above or by clicking **Close** after right-clicking the Taskbar icon.

Speech Recognition

To use this feature, you need to have the sound facility set up and working on your computer, with speakers and a microphone. **Speech Recognition** allows you to control the computer by spoken commands; tasks such as starting programs and opening menus, dictating text and writing and sending e-mails can be accomplished without using the mouse or keyboard at all. First you need to learn a list of spoken commands, by following the Windows Vista **Speech Tutorial**; you must also "train" the computer to recognise your voice and any dialect, if necessary.

The **Speech Recognition** feature is launched by clicking **Start, Control Panel** and then selecting **Speech Recognition Options**. With the **Control Panel** in **Classic View**, this involves double-clicking the icon shown on the right. In **Control Panel Home** you need to  select **Ease of Access** and then **Speech Recognition Options** as shown below.

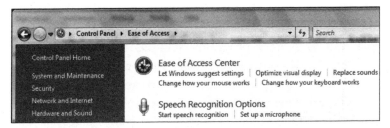

The **Speech Recognition Options** window opens, as shown on the next page; a microphone icon appears on the Taskbar at the bottom right of the screen, indicating that **Speech Recognition** is up and running.

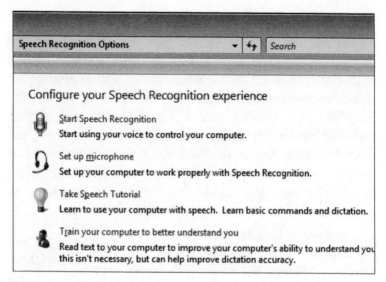

When you first start **Speech Recognition** you are given advice on the use of the microphone and you are asked to read in a piece of sample text. The **Speech Tutorial** helps you to practise all of the basic spoken commands such as **Start Listening, New Line, New Paragraph** and **Correct**. You are given practice at correcting mistakes on the screen and shown how to select menus such as **Start, All Programs** and **File** and to launch programs such as Word using voice commands. If you select **Train your computer to better understand you** shown above, you are given extensive practice exercises in which you speak into the microphone, while the computer learns to recognise your voice.

After you've finished training yourself (and the computer) you are ready to click **Start Speech Recognition** as shown above; this displays the **microphone user interface** shown below:

The user gives commands such as **Start listening** to make the computer begin interpreting the commands spoken into the microphone. The microphone button shown on the left below changes colour – blue indicating the computer is listening to you, grey indicating not listening. The small window in the centre gives text feedback such as **Listening** or **Sleeping**. The message **What was that?** shown in the text window indicates that a command was not understood.

If this occurs you should try giving the command again or try a new command. You can display a list of commands on the screen at any time by saying **What can I say?**

The command **Show numbers** applies numbers which appear transparently over objects on the screen. For example, if the **Show numbers** command allocated the number **14** to a photograph listed in the Windows Explorer, the spoken command **double-click 14** would open the photograph in its associated program, such as Adobe Photoshop Elements.

The Windows Vista Speech Recognition feature will enable many people who can't manipulate a mouse or a keyboard to utilise programs such as Word or Works or e-mail. Using spoken commands, they can create, edit, save and print their own documents. I have found it quite easy to use the Speech Recognition system to dictate fairly simple documents. It is important to work through the tutorials conscientiously and to spend plenty of time training the computer to recognise your voice. It also helps to speak slowly and clearly into the microphone.

Further Help

There are many companies and organisations offering more specialist help than is provided by the tools available within Windows Vista, just discussed. For example, alternative input devices are available for sufferers of illnesses such as Parkinson's Disease or Cerebral Palsy. As mentioned earlier, there is a link, shown below, at the end of the **Ease of Access Recommended settings** in Windows Vista.

Learn about additional assistive technologies online

Clicking this link enables you to access a wide range of information on assistive or accessibility issues. There are also links to the Web sites of companies providing specialist devices, such as, for example, the **Head Mounted Mousing Alternative** link below.

Tracker 2000 - Head Mounted Mousing Alternative by Madentec Limited
"Great for Those with Limited Mobility" More

You can also carry out your own Internet search for help by entering relevant keywords, such as **disability computer technology** or **special needs computer equipment** or **computer accessibility** into a search engine such as Google.

Click on any of the links (which appear underlined in the list of search results) to view the relevant Web site.

Getting Online

Introduction

This chapter describes how a PC computer running Windows Vista can be connected to the Internet, so that you can carry out activities such as finding information from Web pages, sending and receiving e-mails and creating your own blogs and Web pages. These activities are discussed in detail later in this book.

In order to connect to the Internet you will need:

- A computer and a modem or a router.
- A telephone line or cable TV line.
- An account with an Internet Service Provider.

Choosing an Internet Service Provider

The first task is to subscribe to an Internet Service Provider (ISP). This is a company which provides your connection to the Internet through their special computers, known as *servers*. The Internet Service Providers also supply pages of news and information and in some cases telephone and television services. Well known ISPs include BT, AOL, Orange, Tiscali, Sky and Virgin Media, for example.

There is a bewildering choice of Internet Service Providers; if you already have access to the Internet there's a wealth of information giving details of the offers available from the various ISPs. Web sites which provide detailed comparisons of ISPs are discussed shortly.

If you don't yet have an Internet connection of any sort, you can find out about different Internet Service Providers by:

- Talking to other people about their experiences with various ISPs.

- Reading advertisements, reports and reviews in newspapers and magazines.

- Searching for information online using an Internet connection in a library, Internet Café or by using a computer belonging to a friend or relative.

Finding Out About ISPs Online

If you type the letters **ISP** into a search program such as Google, a list of Web sites immediately appears, as shown below. *Broadband* dominates the list of ISPs, an indication of the decline in the use of the earlier *dial-up* modem for connecting to the Internet.

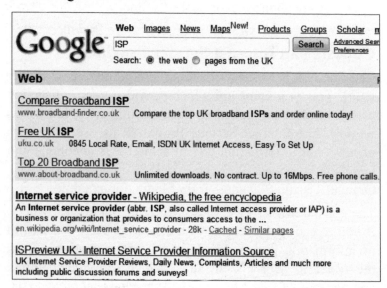

Click on the links shown in the previous list of search results to display the Web sites. The Web sites include much information about the packages on offer from the various Internet Service Providers, as shown below.

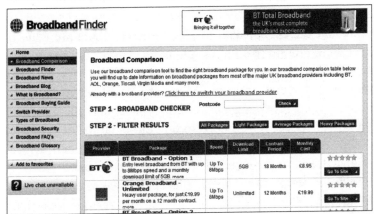

Geographical Location

Some of the Web sites found in the previous **ISP** search allow you to enter your post code to find services available in your particular area. A few remote areas of the United Kingdom still can't get broadband through a local telephone exchange. Conversely a search in some areas will show that *cable broadband* is available from Virgin Media, (formerly ntl:Telewest). This uses television cables as the medium, rather than BT telephone lines.

In some areas Internet Service Providers have installed their own broadband equipment in BT telephone exchanges. This may enable them to offer a cheaper service and is known as *local loop unbundling (LLU)*.

Web sites worth looking at include:

www.broadband-finder.co.uk   **www.uswitch.com**

www.ispreview.co.uk   **www.top10-broadband.co.uk**

Criteria for Choosing an ISP

Download Speed

This is a measure of the speed in *megabits* per second that you can download files from the Internet. (*Mega* means approximately 1 million; a *bit* is a 0 or a 1, used to represent the digital data in a computer). There are usually several different packages on offer based on price and speed. For example, a speed of up to 2Mbps for £10 per month or a speed of up to 8Mbps at £19.99 per month. For simple Web browsing and e-mail you could manage with the lower speed; if you need to download large files (music, video, etc.) then go for the highest speed you can afford. High speed is also needed to receive *live* music, video or television across the Internet. This is known as *streaming*.

Although download speeds of *up to* 8Mbps and even 24Mbps are quoted, these are *nominal* figures which may not be achieved in your particular situation. For example, performance deteriorates the farther you are from the telephone exchange. Once your broadband is up and running, several Web sites allow you to check the speed of an Internet connection, such as the following:

http://speedtester.bt.com

To have a look at some more of these, type keywords such as **broadband speed tester** into an Internet search program such as Google, etc.

Monthly Costs

These may be as little as £10 for a light user package but may only be for a limited period such as 6 months. An 8Mb package is more likely to be nearer £20 per month or more, at the time of writing. The charge for BT Broadband is billed as part of the normal BT household telephone bill.

Download Limit

This refers to the amount of data (Web pages, music files, etc.), you can download per month. The average user can probably manage with 2GB (gigabytes) per month while anyone downloading lots of music will need more. If you sign up for a certain download limit, expect to pay more for each gigabyte above the limit. Some ISPs offer an unlimited downloading facility (at a price).

Contract Period

Most Internet Service Providers require you to sign up for their service for a minimum of 12 or 18 months, with a financial penalty if you cancel the contract early.

Set Up Costs

ISPs usually talk you through the set up process for free; others may charge perhaps £30-£50. Often it involves no more than telephone support, though some ISPs may offer the services of an engineer to complete the installation.

Free Modem

Some packages offer a free or reduced price modem when you sign up. If you only intend to use one computer, a single *ADSL (Asymmetric Digital Subscriber Line) modem* or cable modem will suffice. If you have more than one computer, or want to use a laptop computer around your home, a *wireless router* is a good choice. These are offered free by some ISPs.

BT is also currently offering 250 minutes a month access to 10,000 Wi-Fi (wireless) "hotspots", Internet access points in hotels, restaurants, stations and airports for laptop users on the move. Free Internet telephone calls from your computer may also be on offer as well as online safe storage capacity for your photos or important files.

Connection Time

There is usually a delay between taking out a broadband contract and being able to connect to the service. In the case of BT you need to wait about a week for the telephone line to be *activated* or "broadband enabled".

Dial-up Internet Connections

The dial-up modem, also known as the 56K modem, has been overtaken in many homes by much faster broadband technology. The main disadvantages of dial-up are:

- It is much slower than broadband.

- Your computer literally has to dial a telephone number every time you connect to the Internet during the day (broadband stays connected all day).

- You can't use a telephone handset at the same time as the Internet, on a single telephone line (as you can with broadband).

However, you might choose to use dial-up for one or more of the following reasons:

- A broadband service may not be available in your part of the country.

- Your budget may not stretch to the set-up costs and monthly subscription for broadband.

- You don't need to download large files such as music, etc.

- You are not too bothered if Web pages are found and displayed relatively slowly.

You can find out about the dial-up services offered by ISPs after doing a search for **dial-up** in a program like Google, as shown below.

As can be seen above, some of the ISPs offer a "free" dial-up service; this means there is no monthly subscription, you just pay for the time you spend connected. With dial-up, your modem "calls" a telephone number to connect to an ISP *server*. You can actually hear the number being dialled. Always check with the ISP that these calls are charged at the *local* telephone call rate.

The time spent on the Internet will show up as part of your telephone bill; if the ISP is not the provider of the telephone line, they will receive a portion of your payment.

The "free" service may also make money by charging you for telephone support (perhaps 50p or £1 per minute). You may also be bombarded with "pop up" adverts.

Pay As You Go

If you are a light user of the Internet (under 5 hours per week, say) the "pay as you go" option will work out cheaper.

Unlimited Use

Heavy users wanting unlimited access can expect to pay a monthly subscription of about £15 or more for a dial-up connection – dearer than some broadband services.

Daytime

Limited to certain daytime hours, for a lower monthly fee.

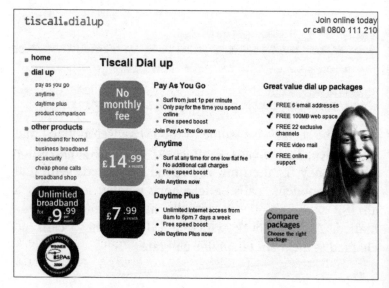

Checklist for Choosing an ISP

The following list may be helpful when choosing an Internet Service Provider:

- Speed and reliability for connecting to the Internet.

- The download speed. This will determine the time for Web pages to open on the screen and for large files to be copied down to your computer.

- The monthly download limit in gigabytes – a measure of how much you use a broadband connection before being charged extra.

- Unlimited access or "pay as you go" (dial-up).

- The monthly subscription charges.

- The minimum contract period.

- Free modem or router included in the package.

- The number of e-mail addresses per account.

- The quality and cost of telephone support.

- The initial setup costs.

- The quality and quantity of any content – Web pages containing news, sport, travel, weather, etc.

- The amount of Web space provided free for subscribers to create their own Web sites.

- Virus protection in e-mails and file downloads.

- Firewalls to prevent illegal access to your computer.

- Filters to remove "junk" mail.

- Parental (and grandparents') control over children's access to inappropriate Web sites.

- For dial-up, telephone access numbers available at *local* telephone rates (does not apply to broadband).

Everything You Need
Username and password
Once you've subscribed to an Internet Service Provider you will be provided with a *username* and *password*. The ISP may give you a temporary password which you can change later; in situations where security is important you are advised to change your password regularly. The ISP will also provide information for setting up your *e-mail* service, discussed in a later chapter in this book.

Modem or Router
If you buy a new computer it may already have a dial-up modem built-in. Many broadband services include a modem router free or at a discount price. In the case of broadband using a BT telephone line, you will have to wait until the line is *activated* for ADSL broadband; this may take about a week.

Connecting the modem or router is not difficult and detailed instructions and all necessary cables will be provided by the ISP or by the modem/router manufacturer. The cable end connections are designed so that you can't fit the cables incorrectly. This genuinely is a job that anyone can do without any technical skills.

Dial-up Modem
As mentioned earlier, the dial-up modem is rapidly being eclipsed as the most popular Internet connection; the main justifications for sticking with dial-up would be because broadband is not available in your area or because your budget does not allow for the extra cost of broadband.

On-board dial-up modem
The on-board modem in which all of the components are built into the *motherboard* i.e. the main circuit board inside of the computer's case.

Dial-up Modem on an Expansion Card

The dial-up modem can be in the form of an expansion card, a small circuit board which pushes into a slot on the computer's motherboard. An example of an expansion card is shown on page 108.

Both of the modems above take their power off the computer and therefore don't need a separate power supply.

The External Dial-up Modem

This is a stand-alone device, with its own power supply cable. A special cable connects the modem to one of the *COM* ports (labelled *COM1* and *COM2*) on the back of the computer. The external modem has a series of diagnostic lights; for example, telling you when the power is on and when data is being transmitted, etc.

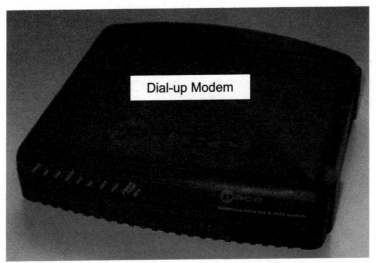

Dial-up Modem

All you need for the three dial-up modems on the previous page is a single cable (usually provided with the modem) to connect the modem to a standard telephone adaptor containing two sockets. As stated before, you can't use this phone line for ordinary telephone calls while connected to the Internet via a dial-up modem.

After some time the connection with a dial-up modem will usually be terminated either by the user or by the ISP. So you may need to carry out the process of connecting to the Internet by dialling up several times in a day. Compare this with broadband; you go online each morning and it stays connected all day.

The ADSL Modem

ADSL stands for *Asymmetric Digital Subscriber Line*. It is called *asymmetric* because the speed to *download* data (from an Internet server to your computer) is different from the *upload* speed (the speed at which you can send files from your computer to an Internet server.)

ADSL Modem

One cable connects the ADSL modem to one of the computer's USB ports. (USB ports are shown on page 25). Another cable connects the ADSL modem to the broadband telephone line via a special *ADSL filter* or *microfilter* shown below. The filter allows the telephone line to be simultaneously used for the Internet and a telephone call.

Sharing an Internet Connection
The Wireless (Wi-Fi) Router

The latest wireless routers (as shown on the next page) have an ADSL modem built into them. A router enables several computers to share a single Internet connection. The router has its own power supply cable. A single cable connects the router to the broadband telephone line via a microfilter.

The wireless router enables a network to be formed between computers each fitted with a *wireless adaptor* in the form of an *expansion card* or a *dongle*, mentioned in Chapter 2.

Wireless Router

The wireless router usually has some *Ethernet* sockets on the back. These allow several computers to be connected to the router using special Ethernet cables.

To connect computers wirelessly, each computer must be fitted with a *wireless network adaptor*, which may be fitted as an expansion card with its own aerial, as shown below.

Wireless Network Adaptor and Aerial

Alternatively a wireless network adaptor may take the form
of a *dongle*, as shown on the
right. This plugs into a USB
port on the back of the
computer, as shown on page
25. A desktop stand and
extension cable may be used
to allow the wireless dongle to be moved to a position to
give optimum signal strength. The router package usually
includes some Ethernet cables and these are also readily
available from computer shops. A wireless router allows
you to create a home network using a mixture of wireless
and Ethernet connections.

During the initial setting up process, a computer must be
used to run the setup CD. The router is connected to the
computer using either:

- A special USB cable from the router to a USB port
  on the computer.
- An Ethernet cable from the router to an Ethernet
  socket on the computer.

The Ethernet cable is
generally regarded as the
best way of connecting the
router to a computer for the
initial set-up process.
Ethernet cables can be
obtained or made up in
various lengths; an 8 metre
Ethernet cable is shown on the right above.

Once the router is set up, any computer fitted with a
wireless adaptor can connect to the Internet from anywhere
in the home. The wireless network can, if you wish,
function without the Ethernet cable used in the initial setup.

Wi-Fi Range

Ranges of 50 – 300 metres from the router are often quoted by manufacturers but the range and signal strength are affected by obstructions such as walls and steel girders; however, you should be able to get a good Wi-Fi signal around most of an average sized house, flat and garden.

On our small network at home we have one machine next to the router connected by an Ethernet cable; three other machines plus a laptop can be used anywhere in the house or garden through wireless connections. Although the performance of wireless networking is not quite as fast as networking using Ethernet cables, we have found it perfectly satisfactory for surfing the Internet, e-mail and downloading large music and software files. You can also print from any computer to a single printer serving the whole network.

Many people now use a wireless router to connect a single computer to the Internet; in this book, a single computer setup will be referred to as a *wireless network* in addition to the more usual wireless network of two or more computers.

Secure Wi-Fi Networks

If a neighbour has a wireless router, you may detect their network on your computer. Internet "savvy" students and even criminals outside of your home could go online using the Internet connection you are paying for. They might also look at your files of personal and financial information.

The BT Home Hub wireless router uses a string of 10 letters and digits as a *wireless key*. The BT wireless key is printed on a label on the back of the Home Hub router.
The first time you use a computer to connect to the router you must enter the wireless key.

The computer "remembers" the key for subsequent connections. Anyone using a different computer can't connect to the Internet via your router unless they enter the wireless key.

In the example below, my computer is connected to our BT Home Hub.

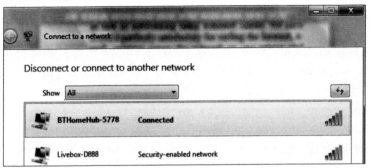

As shown above, my computer has also detected a neighbour's **Livebox** wireless network. If I click the **Livebox** network listed above, I will be unable to connect without entering the **Livebox security key** or **passphrase**.

Security keys such as these should prevent hackers from connecting to your wireless Internet connection.

Wi-Fi Hotspots

There are thousands of Wi-Fi *hotspots* or Internet *access points* in hotels, holiday cottages, stations, airports, etc. Modern laptops have a built-in wireless adaptor. To connect to the Internet, simply take the laptop within range of the hotspot and enter your username and password. With BT Total Broadband, you get several thousand minutes of free connection time per year on the BT Openzone network, with 10,000 hotspots in the UK and Ireland.

www.btopenzone.com

Networking Using Cables Instead of Wireless

You can connect two or more computers to share the Internet using Ethernet cables rather than wireless adapters. This was the standard method for creating *local area networks* in offices, factories, schools and colleges, before the advent of cheap and reliable wireless networking. Cabled networks still have the edge on wireless as far as speed is concerned. On the down side, apart from the physical presence of cables all round your home, a cabled network usually requires holes to be drilled to allow the cables to run through walls and ceilings, etc.

Each computer must have an *Ethernet network adaptor,* nowadays fitted as standard on most new computers. If not, separate Ethernet *network cards*, as shown below, can be bought quite cheaply and pushed into a slot in the computer's motherboard.

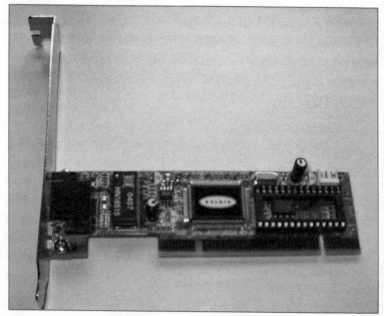

Connecting for the First Time

You should have an installation guide from your ISP or router/modem manufacturer telling you how to connect the various cables. The ISP must also provide you with:

- A username
- A password
- Telephone number (dial-up modem only).

Your Internet Service Provider should also provide a setup CD; insert the CD into your computer, entering your user name and password and following the instructions on the screen. Alternatively you can set up the connection using Windows Vista by clicking **Start** and **Connect To** and choosing the type of network you are creating, as shown below.

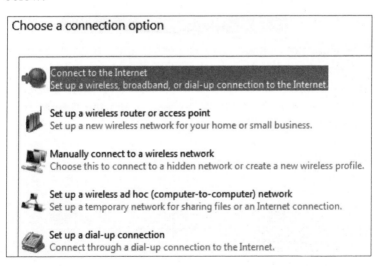

From now on it's just a case of clicking **Next** and following the step-by-step instructions on the screen.

Once you are connected to the Internet, the *network icon* (depicting two monitors) appears in the *notification area* at the right of the Windows Vista Taskbar as shown below.

If you hold the mouse cursor over this icon, a small window appears as shown below. In this example the computer is connected to the Internet and also some **Local** computers.

If you are not connected, a red cross appears over the icon and **Not Connected** is displayed in the above window. To find out more about your Internet connection, *right-click* over the icon and select **Network and Sharing Center** from the pop-up menu. Also click **View status** as shown below.

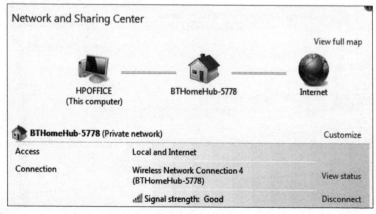

Exploring the Internet

Introduction

A *Web browser* is a program used to navigate around the Internet, viewing Web pages, obtaining information and downloading files. Windows Vista includes its own built-in browser, Internet Explorer 7. Version 7 is the latest in a line of Internet Explorers and incorporates many attractive new features which make it very powerful yet easy to use. Users of Windows XP, the predecessor to Windows Vista, can also upgrade to Internet Explorer 7 by a free download from the Microsoft Web site or as an *automatic update,* discussed later.

Internet Explorer 7 can be launched by clicking the **Start** orb at the bottom left of the screen, then clicking **Internet Explorer** from the Start Menu which appears.

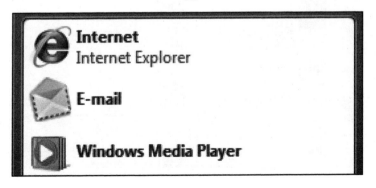

Another way to launch Internet Explorer 7 is to click the Internet Explorer icon on the Quick Launch toolbar at the left of the Taskbar at the bottom left of the screen, as shown below.

Yet another quick way to launch Internet Explorer 7 is to press the **Home** key on your keyboard.

After launching Internet Explorer 7 your computer should quickly connect to the Internet and open your Home Page. While browsing the Internet you can always return to your Home Page by clicking the Home icon, shown left, on the Command Bar towards the top right of the screen, as shown below.

You can set any Web page to be your Home Page and this is discussed shortly. A typical Home Page is shown below:

Clickable Links

The MSN Web site used as the Home Page in the previous screenshot includes several advertisements and news items in various categories. If you move the mouse cursor about the screen, as the cursor passes over certain objects, the cursor changes from an arrow head to a hand. Also when the cursor passes over certain pieces of text, the text becomes underlined and changes colour. The hand and underlined text indicate that the text is a clickable *link* or *hyperlink* to another Web page. A picture can also be used as a link, again indicated by the cursor changing to a hand when you point at the picture.

Links allow you to move from page to page on the Internet, between different pages on the current Web site. Alternatively a link may lead to pages on a totally different Web site stored on a server on the other side of the world. Links are one of the essential tools for "surfing" or browsing the Internet to find information.

The Zoom Feature

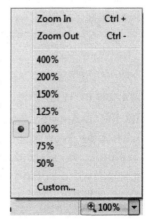

If you can't see the text or graphics very well in Internet Explorer 7, click the downward pointing arrow head at the bottom right of the screen. This opens up the zoom menu shown on the right. Click a % enlargement, or enter your own **Custom Zoom** as a percentage or use the **Ctrl** key with the **+** and **–** keys to **Zoom In** and **Zoom Out**.

Navigating Between Web Pages

The Toolbar across the top of Internet Explorer 7 contains the tools needed for you to "surf the net" by navigating between different Web pages and Web sites. The left-hand group of Toolbar tools is shown below.

Across the top of the Toolbar is the Title, summarizing the currently selected Web page. On the left of the Toolbar are the Forward and Back buttons, allowing you to switch between recently visited pages. The small arrowhead to the right of the Forward and Back buttons shown on the right above presents a dropdown list of recently visited pages.

To the right of the Forward and Back buttons, the Address Bar shown below displays the full Web address of the site you are currently viewing.

http://www.thistleyhaugh.co.uk/attractions.htm

The Web address also goes by the rather unwieldy title of *Uniform Resource Locator*, normally shortened to *URL*.

Names of Web Pages

In the example above **attractions.htm** is the name of a particular Web *page*. The name of the Web *site* in this example is **www.thistleyhaugh.co.uk**. These names are given by the person who created the Web site. The Home Page, i.e. the first page you see when you connect to the Internet, is often given the special name **index.htm**.

You can move to another Web site by clicking in the Address Bar, typing the address and pressing the **Enter** or **Return** key on the keyboard. You might use this method if you had obtained a Web address from an advertisement in a newspaper, for example. Web addresses are discussed in more detail shortly.

Two icons on the left of the Toolbar help you to re-visit pages from previous sessions.

The right-hand icon shown above consists of a green cross superimposed on a yellow star. If you think you might want to revisit the current Web page in the future, click this icon to bookmark the Web page. This launches a small menu which includes the option **Add to Favorites....** Click this option to place a link to the current Web site in your list of bookmarks or **Favorites** (American spelling).

To access your list of favourite Web sites click the yellow star icon shown on the left of the two icons above. This opens the **Favorites Center**, from which the **Favorites** button shown below should be selected. The entries in the **Favorites** list are clickable links which allow you to return to a particular Web site at any time in the future.

Referring to the **Favorites Center** shown at the bottom of the previous page, to the right of the **Favorites** icon is the **Feeds** icon. Feeds are a new feature introduced in Internet Explorer 7 and consist of news and other information which is updated and displayed at regular intervals. Feeds are discussed in more detail shortly.

The **History** feature in the **Favorites Center** shown at the bottom of the previous page keeps a record of all of the sites you have visited recently. Click the **History** button shown below to open up the list of recently-visited sites.

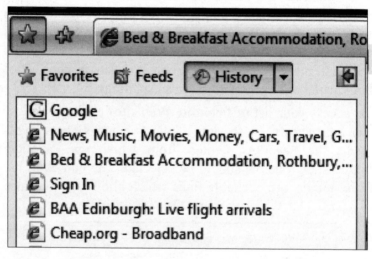

Click on an entry in the list above to return to that Web site. The arrow head to the right of **History** above presents a menu with options to rearrange the list of sites in different orders, i.e. date, alphabetical order, most visited, etc.

The small icon on the right of the Favorites Center "pins" the Center to the screen so that it stays open while you browse various sites in your Favorites or History lists.

Tabbed Browsing

This is a new feature introduced in Internet Explorer 7 and enables you to open several Web sites in one Window at the same time. Previous versions of Internet Explorer required you to open a separate window for each Web site. Clicking the tabs makes it very easy to switch between Web sites, especially useful when you need to keep referring back to different pages for information.

In the example below, three tabs are open in a single Explorer window.

Clicking the first tab, **News, Music, Movies, Mo...** displays the Home Page on this particular computer. The second tab, **Live Search: Orchid** lists the results of a search for the key word **Orchid**, which was entered into the Live Search program, discussed shortly. The third tab above, **all about orchids and h...** is a Web page obtained by clicking one of the links in the search results displayed by the second tab.

To the left of the three tabs shown above is the **Quick Tabs** button. Click the **Quick Tabs** button to see a miniature view or "thumbnail" of the tabbed Web pages, as shown below.

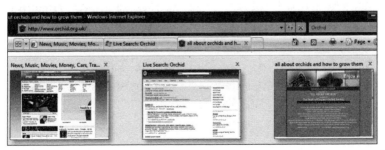

When you click the arrow head to the right of
the **Quick Tabs** button shown on the right, a
list of the tabbed Web pages appears as shown
below.

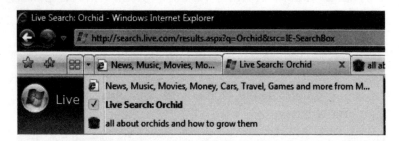

Click an item in the list as shown above to display a
particular Web page.

Opening New Tabbed Web Pages

When you start Internet Explorer, your Home Page is
displayed on a tab. To the right of this tab is a
small blank tab; allow your cursor to hover over
the blank tab and the **New Tab** icon appears, as
shown on the right and below.

Clicking this icon opens a window entitled **Welcome to
Tabbed Browsing**, giving help on opening new tabbed web
pages. There is a box you can click so that the Welcome
window doesn't appear in future. If you now click the
Close button on the Welcome window, a **Blank Page** tab is
displayed, as shown below.

The Blank Page can now be used to open a new tabbed Web page. This can be achieved in the following ways:

- Press the **Ctrl** key while clicking a link on another Web page.

- After typing an address into the Address Bar, (discussed on pages 114 and 115), hold down the **Alt** key and press the **Enter** key, also known as the **Return** key.

- After entering a key word in the Search bar, hold down the **Alt** key and press the **Enter** key. The list of results of the search will appear as a Web page with its own tab.

- Double-click a shortcut icon for the Web page on the Windows desktop.

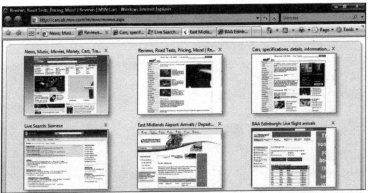

A single click on any of the thumbnail versions of the Web pages above displays the page in full.

To close an individual tabbed Web page, right-click over the tab and click **Close** or click the cross on the **Quick Tabs** thumbnail. To close all of the tabs click the **Close** cross on the Internet Explorer 7 window, as shown on the right.

Several important features are found on the right-hand side of the Internet Explorer 7 screen, as shown below.

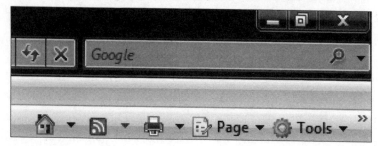

Maximizing, Minimizing and Closing Windows

Three icons at the top right of the screen are used to Minimize, Maximize or Close a window, reading from left to right. Minimizing a window reduces it to an icon and a title on the Taskbar at the bottom of the screen. In Windows Vista, passing the cursor over the icon on the Taskbar displays a large thumbnail view of the window, as shown below.

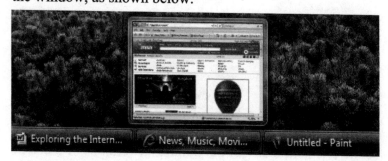

Click the Taskbar icon to display the window full size. The Maximize button makes a window fill the whole screen. Then the Restore button (shown in the middle of the screenshot on the right) is displayed, enabling the window to be returned to its original size.

Searching for Information

The Instant Search bar towards the top right of the Internet Explorer 7 window is used for finding Web pages which contain certain keywords.

Suppose you wanted to find out about the **Atlantic Salmon**. The keywords, chosen by you to uniquely identify your subject, are entered into the search bar as shown below.

When you click the magnifying glass icon as shown above, or press the **Enter** or **Return** key, a list of results fills the screen. In this example, thousands of Web pages are found, all containing the words **atlantic** and **salmon**. The first few search results are shown below.

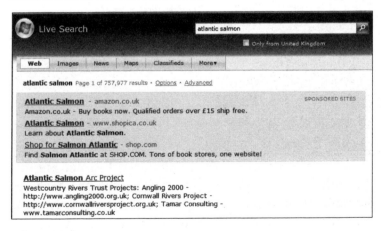

SPONSORED SITES are Web sites published by companies who pay to be listed near the top of the search results.

The list of search results shown on the previous page contains "clickable" links to Web sites which all include the keywords **atlantic** and **salmon** somewhere within their pages. The clickable links are underlined, as shown below.

Atlantic Salmon Trust | Welcome
An organisation working to conserve **Atlantic salmon** and sea trout.
www.**atlanticsalmon**trust.org · Cached page

Click on a link, as shown underlined above, to open up the relevant Web site. If you hold down the **Ctrl** key while clicking the link, the Web page opens in a new tab, as mentioned earlier in this chapter.

The search usually places the most relevant results at the top of the list. So you'll often find the information you need just by looking at the Web sites listed in the first few pages of the results.

Narrowing a Search

There are many ways to narrow down a search to eliminate irrelevant results. For example, enclosing the keywords in inverted commas or speech marks, e.g. "**atlantic salmon**", will find only those Web pages where the keywords occur together, in that specific order – not scattered separately about a Web site. Adding extra keywords will also narrow the search and eliminate some of the irrelevant results.

Cached Pages

Sometimes you may click an underlined link and find the Web site is not available. This may be due to a technical problem or possibly because the site is currently being updated. Clicking the **Cached page** link shown in the screenshot above displays an earlier version of the Web page. Although perhaps not completely up-to-date, the cached page may still contain some useful information.

Alternative Search Programs

Internet Explorer 7 allows you to change the search program or search "engine" as they are often called. This is the program listed in the Instant Search bar and is used to find the information you are interested in. If you click the downward pointing arrow head to the right of the magnifying glass shown below, a drop-down menu lists the search programs currently installed. **Google**, listed below, is probably the world's most popular search program and is an essential tool for many people. **Live Search** is the search program provided with Internet Explorer 7.

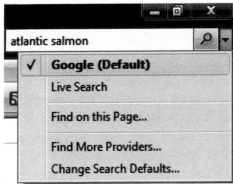

If you select **Find More Providers...** shown above, a list of search programs tailored for various searching purposes is displayed, together with instructions for adding a new search program to the Instant Search menu shown above.

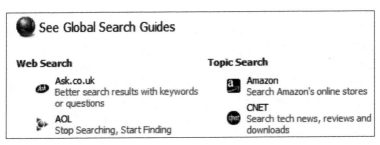

The final group of icons on the right of the screen is known as the Command Bar and is shown below.

The Home Page

The Home Page is the page which opens each time you start Internet Explorer 7. You can choose which page to set as your Home Page, as discussed shortly. When you've been browsing around lots of Web sites, clicking the Home button shown on the right returns you to your Home Page.

Changing Your Home Page

Make sure the Web page you want to use as your new Home Page is open on the screen. Then click the downward pointing arrow head to the right of the Home icon, and select **Add or Change Home Page...** from the menu which appears. This causes the **Add or Change Home Page** dialogue box to open, as shown below. Please note that you can make the current Web page your new Home Page or alternatively the currently selected *tab set* of Web pages.

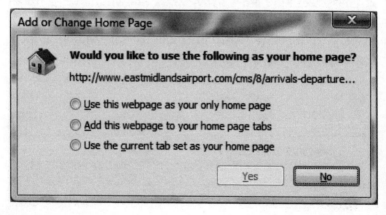

RSS Feeds

The icon shown on the right and at the top of the previous page represents a new feature known as *RSS feeds*. RSS is an abbreviation for *Really Simple Syndication*. An RSS feed is similar to a newsflash, in which regularly updated information, such as the news and weather, is downloaded to your computer. When you visit a Web site which can supply RSS feeds, the icon shown above becomes coloured. Clicking the coloured icon opens the feed, as shown in the extract below from the feeds provided by the BBC Weather Centre.

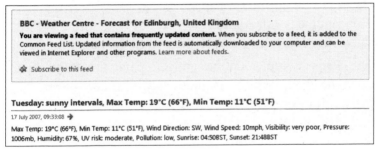

The feed is really a quick summary, in a simplified format, of the very latest key facts from a Web site. To subscribe to this feed and obtain regular updates from the site, click the above link, **Subscribe to this feed**. (Subscribing is usually free). To view a feed you have already subscribed to, open the **Favorites Center** discussed earlier, click the **Feeds** button and then click the name of the feed, as shown below.

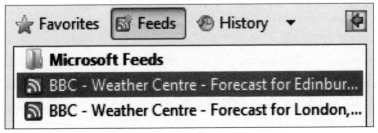

Printing Web Pages

To send the current Web page directly to your printer without altering any settings, click the printer icon on the right-hand side of the screen.

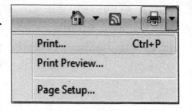

If you click the downward pointing arrow to the right of the printer icon you can select **Print Preview...**, showing how the page will appear on paper. This includes an option to shrink the contents of a Web page to fit the paper.

The **Page Setup...** option above opens the **Page Setup** dialogue box, which includes settings for paper size, printing in **Portrait** or **Landscape** orientation and the ability to add or remove page **Headers** and **Footers**.

Saving a Web Page

Click the **Page** icon shown above and enter a suitable **File name** in the **Save Webpage** dialogue box shown below. This places a copy of the Web on your computer's hard disc, in your **Downloads** folder by default.

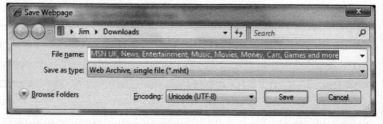

To open the saved Web page at a later date, double-click its entry in the folder in which it was saved.

The Tools Menu

Clicking the **Tools** icon on the Command Bar opens the menu shown below. The main options are discussed below and elsewhere in this book.

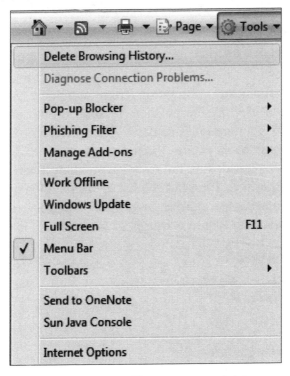

Delete Browsing History... allows you to delete records in your **History** feature, in the **Favorites Center** discussed earlier. These are links to Web sites you have visited previously. You can also choose to delete **Temporary Internet Files** and **Cookies**. These are temporary files which accumulate as a result of your Internet surfing and may clog your system if not removed periodically.

The Pop-up Blocker

Pop-ups are small windows which suddenly appear on your screen, usually advertising a product or service and they are often a nuisance. The **Pop-up Blocker** can be set to give various levels of prevention such as to block most pop-ups but allow those from certain Web sites.

The Phishing Filter

Phishing is a modern type of fraud in which criminals try to obtain financial information from computer users. One approach used by the phishers is to send out e-mails with links to genuine-looking bank Web sites, asking you to enter your bank details. Banks never ask you to provide your personal details online. The **Phishing Filter** checks a suspicious Web site against a list of sites known or reported to be used by phishers and if necessary issues an appropriate on-screen warning.

Check This Website	Phishing Filter
Turn Off Automatic Website Checking...	Manage Add-ons
Report This Website	Work Offline
Phishing Filter Settings	Windows Update

Windows Update

This is a method by which Microsoft sends Windows modifications direct to your computer via the Internet. Updates may be improvements in security or corrections to overcome "bugs". When you click **Windows Update** from the menu on the previous page there is an option to **Change settings**. You can choose to schedule updates to be installed automatically every day. Alternatively you can decide whether or not to install individual updates.

Full Screen on the menu
shown earlier and on the
right expands the
Internet Explorer 7
window to fill the whole

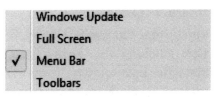

screen. **Full Screen** can easily be switched on (and off) by
pressing the **F11** key near the top of the keyboard.

The **Menu Bar** option shown above causes a traditional
Menu Bar to be displayed, as shown below, starting with
File and **Edit**, etc.

Drop-down menus are opened by clicking **File**, **Edit**, **View**,
Favorites, **Tools** or **Help**. The drop-down menus can be
used as an alternative to the new icons introduced in
Internet Explorer 7 and described on the previous pages.

The Status Bar

The **Toolbars** option shown at the top right of this page and
on the **Tools** menu on page 127 allows you to display
features such as **Favorites**, **Feeds**, **History** and the **Status
Bar**. The **Status Bar** near the bottom of the screen gives the
progress during tasks such as downloading a Web page.

Downloading picture http://www.forestry.gov.uk/images/

Protected Mode

This is intended to prevent malicious software being
installed on your computer from the Internet. To change the
security settings or switch **Protected Mode** on or off,
double-click the icon or the text, shown below, which is
displayed on the right-hand side of the **Status Bar**.

Internet | Protected Mode: On

129

Internet Options

This is the last option shown on the **Tools** menu on page 127. Clicking this option launches the **Internet Options** dialogue box shown below. This allows you to tailor Internet Explorer to your own requirements if you are not happy with the default settings.

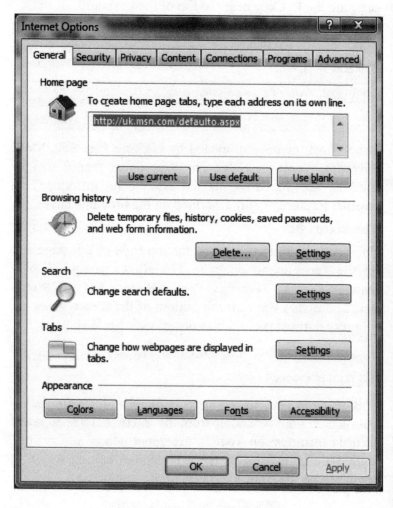

Using the Address Bar to Connect to a Web Site

To use this method of navigating to a Web site, you obviously need to obtain the address first, perhaps from an advertisement, or newspaper article. Every Web site has a unique address, such as **http://www.mycompany.co.uk/**. This can be entered manually into the **Address** bar of the Web browser, as shown below.

Do not enter the address into a search bar such as Google.

In computing jargon, the address of a Web site is known as a *URL* or *Uniform Resource Locator*. In the above example, the meanings of the parts of the address are as follows:

http:

HyperText Transfer Protocol. This is a set of rules used by Web servers. **ftp** is another protocol used for transferring files across the Internet.

www

This means the site is part of the World Wide Web.

mycompany

This is the name of the company or organization hosting the Web site on its server computer.

co.uk

This denotes a Web site owned by a UK company. **co** is known as the *domain type*.

mycompany.co.uk

This part of the Web address is known as the *domain name*.

131

Other common Web site domain types include:

biz   Business

com   Company or Commercial organisation

eu   European Community

info   Information site or service

me.uk UK individual

org   Non-profit making organization

gov   Government

net   Internet company.

In addition, some Web addresses include the code for a country, such as **fr** and **uk** as in:

www.bbc.co.uk/

If you know the address of a Web site, enter this into the address bar at the top of the Web browser as shown below. (In practice you can miss out the **http://** part of the address.)

When you click the **Go** arrow or press **Enter** your browser should connect to the Web site and display its Home Page on the screen.
Then you can start moving about the site using the links within the page as described earlier. If you click the downward pointing arrow head to the left of the **Go** arrow shown above, a drop-down menu appears with a list of the addresses of your recently visited Web sites. If you click one of the addresses it will be placed in the **Address** bar and you can then connect to the Web site by clicking the **Go** arrow.

Web Sites of Special Interest

There are many Web sites containing useful information for older people. The following Web addresses can be typed straight in after clicking in the **Address** bar. There's no need to enter **http://** every time. Most of the Web sites give advice and information on topics such as health, insurance, travel and finance for the over 50s.

www.50plusexpeditions.com World-wide adventure travel.

www.ageconcern.org.uk Age Concern Web Site.

www.agepartnership.co.uk Equity release specialists.

www.agepositive.gov.uk Focus on skills, ability, not age.

www.arp.org.uk Association of Retired Persons over 50.

www.cennet.co.uk Lifestyles for the over 50s.

www.cornhilldirect.co.uk Insurance for the over 50s.

www.direct.gov.uk Guide to government services.

www.dwp.gov.uk Advice on benefits, work and pensions.

www.fiftyplus.co.uk Fashion catalogue for women over 50.

www.friendsreunited.com Catch up with old school friends.

www.hairnet.co.uk Digital Unite (DU) (formerly Hairnet) – computer training for the over 50s.

www.helptheaged.org.uk Support for older people.

www.kelkoo.co.uk Price checks on Internet goods for sale.

www.laterlife.com Promotes a fuller life for the over 50s.

www.moneysupermarket.com Comparisons of prices of goods and services.

www.neighbourhoodwatch.net Promotes home security.

www.nhsdirect.nhs.uk Advice and help with illness.

www.opin.org.uk Older People's Information Network.

www.primeiniative.org.uk Encourages over 50s enterprise.

www.saga.co.uk Wide range of services for older people.

www.seniority.co.uk Internet community for over 50s.

www.seniorsnetwork.co.uk News and information.

www.ship-ltd.org Release capital tied up in your home.

www.silversurfers.net Provides links to an enormous range of Web sites relevant to over 50s in particular.

www.sixtyplusurfers.co.uk Online magazine for over 60s.

www.theoldie.co.uk A witty magazine for *all* ages.

www.thewillsite.co.uk Help in making your own will.

www.thisismoney.co.uk Guide to savings and loans.

www.travel55.co.uk Holidays for older people.

www.uswitch.com Finds cheapest gas, electricity and phone suppliers in your area.

Finding Information with Google

Introduction

Google is a tool for finding the information you want; it's useful as a starting point for much of our Internet browsing. Google finds highly relevant Web pages to match the *keyword* search criteria you make up and enter into the Google search bar. Clickable links on these Web pages then allow you to navigate to other relevant Web pages.

In addition to the keyword search program, the Google Pack is a collection of free software providing a wide range of tools for information gathering and other activities.

Google was started by two students at Stanford University and has grown into a multi-national corporation on the strength of its ability to find relevant results quickly. This has enabled Google to attract advertising revenues and to expand into other online activities such as maps, news and e-mail. At the time of writing Google is easily the world's most popular search program; it is now so popular that a new verb, "to Google", has entered the English language.

You can start Google straightaway by entering the address **www.google.co.uk** into the Address Bar, as shown below.

 http://www.google.co.uk/

Searching Overview

When you press the **Enter** key, the Google search bar opens in its own Web page as shown below. A flashing cursor appears in the search bar ready for you to start entering your *keyword(s)*. You make up your own keywords to suit the subject you are interested in. For example, to find information about Dr. Johnson of dictionary fame, enter his full name in the Google search bar, as shown below. Please note that it's important to enter Samuel in the Doctor's name, as there will be many other Dr. Johnsons. Otherwise Google will find and list all of these unwanted results.

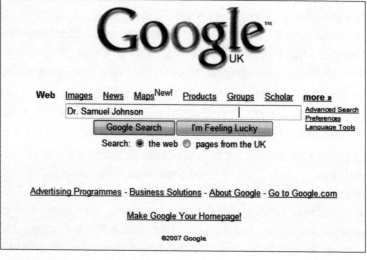

As discussed shortly, after you've entered your chosen keywords, pressing **Enter** on the keyboard or clicking the **Google Search** button will produce a list of results. These results all contain clickable links leading to Web pages relevant to Dr. Samuel Johnson. Once on a Web site, click on further links within the Web pages to navigate to other pages containing information related to Dr. Johnson.

Creating a Desktop Icon for Google

As Google is likely to become a regular tool for much of our Web searching, it's handy to have a Google icon on our Windows Vista Desktop. Simply right-click anywhere on the Google Web page shown on the previous page, then click **Create Shortcut** from the menu which pops up. Now select the **Yes** button from the menu which appears, as shown below.

Clicking **Yes** places a Google icon on the Windows Vista Desktop as illustrated below.

Now whenever you want to start searching for information, simply double-click the Google icon on your desktop. There are several other ways to start Google, including making it your Home Page or making it your default search program in the Instant Search bar discussed in Chapter 7.

Entering Search Criteria into Google

Suppose you want to find out as much as possible about the brilliant orchid family of plants. Start Google and enter the keyword **orchid** into the search bar as shown below.

As we are searching the World Wide Web for pages containing the word **orchid**, **Web** is selected in the row shown above, (starting **Web Images News**, etc.) (Google **Images**, **News** and **Maps** are discussed shortly). The above screenshot shows that we can search the entire Web or confine our search to pages from the UK. This is done by clicking in the small circles, known as *radio buttons*, shown above and below.

Search: ◉ the web ◯ pages from the UK

When you've entered your keyword(s) in the search bar, click the **Google Search** button shown above to begin trawling the billions of Web pages on the World Wide Web. Any Web page containing the keyword(s) will be listed in the results. In practice the results are displayed almost immediately, as shown on the next page. If, instead of the **Google Search** button shown above, you click the **I'm Feeling Lucky** button, Google immediately opens the Web page which would have appeared at the top of the results.

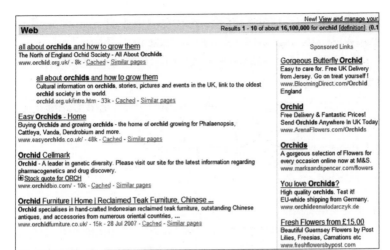

Each entry in the results list above includes a link to a Web page containing the word **orchid**. A staggering 16 million Web pages were found in 0.15 seconds. Click on a link, shown underlined, to open up the corresponding Web page.

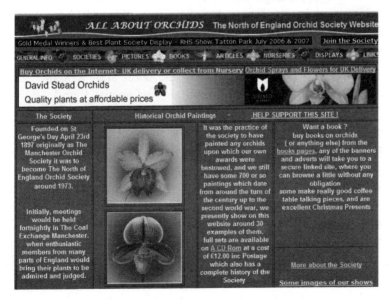

The **Sponsored Links** on the previous list of results lead to the Web sites of commercial companies. They have paid for their links to appear near the top of the list of results.

Cached Pages

Each entry in the results list contains the word **Cached**, as shown below.

all about **orchids** and how to grow them
The North of England Ochid Society - All About **Orchids**.
www.**orchid**.org.uk/ - 8k - Cached - Similar pages

If you click the word **Cached** as shown above, an earlier version of the Web page is displayed. This may be useful if, for some reason, the latest version is not available. As shown above, there is also a link to **Similar pages**.

Narrowing a Search

With over 16 million Web pages found, each containing the word **orchid**, many of the pages involve the word **orchid** in an irrelevant, non-horticultural context. For example, there is a company called **Orchid Furniture** and numerous restaurants with the word orchid in their name.

Adding extra keywords such as **wild** and **British**, for example, greatly reduces the number of results found.

To eliminate from the results, say, all restaurants using the word **orchid** in their title, we add the unwanted word **restaurant** preceded by a minus sign, as shown below.

The Scope of Google

The previous pages showed how Google can search the billions of Web pages on the Internet and immediately find pages containing the keywords we have chosen and entered into the search bar. The amount of information on the Web is phenomenal and far exceeds anything possible in the traditional printed encyclopedia. It is also more up-to-date since Web pages can be amended far more quickly than the time it takes to publish a new edition of a printed encyclopedia. So you can use a program like Google to find a wealth of the latest information on any subject under the sun, by entering a few carefully chosen keywords.

Google Images

There is very much more to Google than the general keyword searching of the Web just discussed. For example, you can target your search at a category, such as **Images**, **News** or **Maps**, as shown below.

For this example, we will continue to use **orchid** as the keyword in the search bar, but this time we will find only images of the plant. Click **Images** above the search bar as shown above.

Now click **Search Images** and the resulting list is made up entirely of pictures of orchids, as shown on the next page. Each small picture or "thumbnail" is a clickable link to a larger version of the picture.

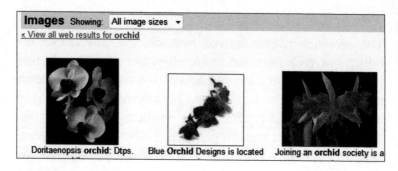

Google News

Selecting **News** from above the Google search bar shown below enables you to produce a listing of the latest news flashes relating to the keyword in the search bar. For example, you might want to find out the latest information on a topical subject such as the severe floods which affected parts of Britain in 2007. Select **News** and enter **UK floods** in the Google search bar, as shown below.

Click on the appropriate link, shown as underlined text, to read the relevant news story.

Google Maps

With **Maps** selected above the Google search bar as shown below, enter into the search bar the name of the place you want to find. Then click the **Search Maps** button as shown below.

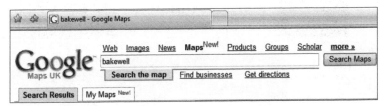

A map of your chosen location appears and there are buttons to zoom in and out and to scroll in four directions. Each location can be displayed in the usual map format with road and street names, or as a satellite view (showing individual houses) or as a

hybrid view combining the two.

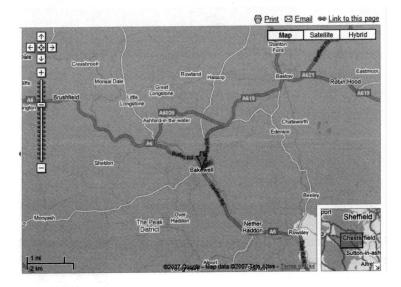

Google Earth

Google Earth is a really impressive program; it allows you to see an image of planet Earth and zoom in on any location you choose. Then you can look at 3D satellite pictures of streets, buildings, rivers and other features. You can experience worldwide places of interest, without leaving home, such as the Pyramids or the Eiffel Tower.

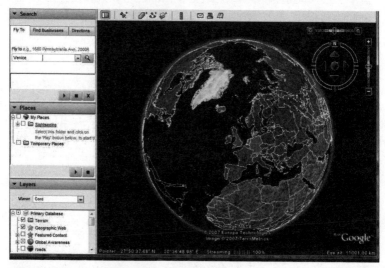

To move directly to a location you can also type a location in the **Fly to** bar on the left-hand side of the screen, in the **Search** panel above and in the extract below.

Powerful navigation tools allow you to zoom in or out of your chosen location and you can tilt and rotate the view and change the centre point of the view.

Google Earth is a powerful program which requires a modern computer; a broadband Internet connection is essential. The program can be downloaded from the Google Website, after clicking **more** as shown below.

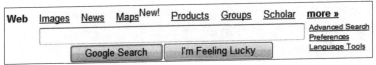

Then from the list of **More Google products** which appears click **Earth**, as shown in the extract below.

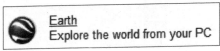

A page appears showing examples of what you can do with Google Earth. Many international organizations use the program to present information on a global scale; for example, to show the spread of Avian Flu across continents. There is also a button allowing you to download a free copy of the program onto your computer.

It's just a case of following the instructions to download and save the program on your hard disc. Initially a file in a compressed format is downloaded. This must be expanded and run to install a working version of Google Earth on your computer. The installation process places an icon for Google on the Vista Desktop. Double-click this icon whenever you want to launch Google Earth.

(Downloading software from the Internet and installing it on your computer is covered in detail in the next chapter.)

Google Earth opens, displaying the full planet as shown on page 144. If you enter a location, such as **Venice**, in the **Fly to** box shown earlier, Google quickly "flies" to the location.

As you zoom into Venice, small camera icons appear on the screen. Clicking a camera icon launches a picture taken from the camera position. If you're preparing for a holiday or deciding where to go, Google Earth allows you to see any location on the globe

Pan⊕ramio

Basilique San Marco Photograph by Philippe Stone

in great detail. If you're unable to travel, Google Earth provides a virtual visit without the need to leave home.

Internet Activities

Introduction

The range of activities which can be carried out over the Internet is enormous. Once you become familiar with using the Internet it's likely to become a major part of your life – you'll probably wonder how you ever managed without it. This chapter looks at some more specific examples of the way the Internet can be used to help with important activities in both leisure and daily life. Without exception these online tasks can be carried out more quickly and easily than by traditional methods.

Many of these tasks involve the transfer of money over the Internet. At the time of writing there is much concern about the way organized crime is trying to exploit any weaknesses in Internet security. It's therefore essential to take Internet security very seriously and this subject is discussed in detail in Chapter 10, Internet Banking and Security. The tasks described in this chapter, which should be of particular interest to older people, include:

- Arranging Holidays
- Internet Shopping
- Tracing Family History
- Downloading Music
- Downloading Software.

Arranging Holidays

Nowadays more of us are using the Internet to arrange our holidays online rather than buying a package from a travel agent. Many hotels and guest houses have their own Web site. With several linked pages, this can provide far more information about the accommodation than an entry in a brochure. Some Web sites provide virtual tours and videos showing you exactly what the accommodation is like.

Using the Internet you can browse through lots of holiday destinations looking at tourist information and pictures of local amenities. Google Earth, described in the last chapter, provides high quality 3D satellite images of any location.

Most resorts, towns and villages now have their own Web site with links to local hotels, enabling you to view the facilities, before booking your holiday online.

For example, if considering a holiday in Cornwall, you might type the keyword **Penzance** into the search bar in a program like Google, as discussed earlier. This particular search produces a list of Web sites, with a link to the site "**Penzance OnLine**" at the top of the list.

Penzance OnLine - complete information source for **Penzance**, centre ...
An information source for the town including shopping, community, tourism, sport, recreation and travel, from **Penzance** Chamber of Commerce.
www.**penzance**.co.uk/ - 11k - Cached - Similar pages
    Tourism in Penzance & West Cornwall - www.penzance.co.uk/tourism/home.htm
    Accommodation in and around ... - www.penzance.co.uk/accommodation/home.htm
    The Complete Information Source ... - www.penzance.co.uk/descrip/index.htm
    Eating Places & Watering Holes - www.penzance.co.uk/eatdrink/home.htm
    More results from www.penzance.co.uk »

As shown above, the Web address of this site is:

www.penzance.co.uk/

If you click the link shown on the results list on the previous page, the **Penzance on line** Web site opens as shown below.

The above site is promoted by the Penzance Chamber of Commerce.

The Web site contains many links to places of interest and amenities in the town and surrounding area, as shown in the enlarged extract on the left.

Select **Where to Stay** and after clicking a further link to **Hotels**, the list of hotels shown on the next page appears.

The Longboat Hotel
Market Jew Street, Penzance. Phone: 01736-364137
Hotel Penzance
Briton's Hill, Penzance. Phone: 01736-363117
Summer House
Cornwall Terrace, Penzance. Phone: 01736-363744
Tarbert Hotel
11 Clarence Street, Penzance. Phone: 01736-363758

For example, selecting the Tarbert Hotel above takes us to the hotel's home page, shown below.

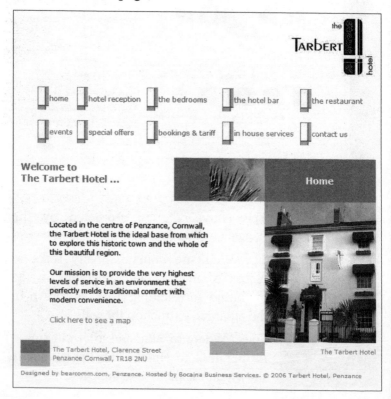

From the home page there are links to all of the facilities of the hotel and also information about events in the area. Click **the bedrooms** link shown on the previous page and samples of the accommodation can be viewed.

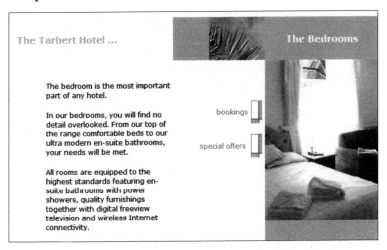

You can also have a look at some sample menus.

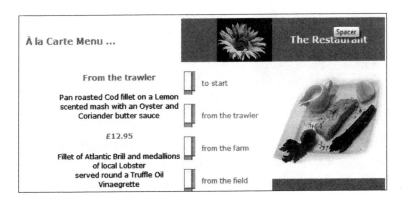

Clicking the **events** button enables you to find out what's on in the surrounding area, as shown in the extract below.

> **AUGUST**
> 4th. Falmouth Classics
> Date TBA. Jazz in the Gardens, Pencarrow
> 11th - 18th. Falmouth Regatta Week
> 17th - 19th. West of England Steam Rally, St Agnes
> 19th - 25th. Fowey Royal Regatta week
> 25th - 27th. Morval Vintage Rally, near Looe
> 27th. Polruan Regatta Day
> 25th - 1st September. Bude Jazz Festival

Finally you can either make an enquiry or a definite booking after clicking the **bookings & tariff** button shown on page 150. Select your **Check-in Date** and accommodation requirements as shown below.

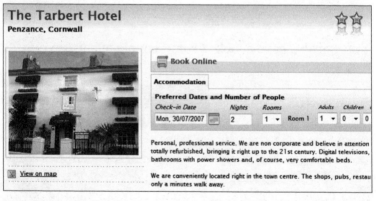

The program checks the availability of your required rooms on your chosen dates and calculates the total cost. If you wish to proceed with the booking it's simply a case of clicking the **Continue** button, agreeing to the hotel's terms and conditions then entering your personal details such as name, address and credit card information.

Booking a Flight

Similar online booking procedures are becoming the norm for holiday flights as well as hotels. If you book a flight online with one of the low cost airlines such as easyJet.com, links on their Web site also enable you to book accommodation, car hire and travel insurance, etc.

If you book your flights online well in advance, you can get some very good low price deals – leave it until the last minute and you may have to pay a lot more. If you're travelling light with only hand luggage, some airlines allow you to check in online – saving you some of the hassle of airport queuing. You need a printer to make a hard copy of your travel documents, which replace the traditional tickets.

Online flight and holiday arrangements can be made from the comfort of your own home, allowing you to see what's available. This should enable you to save time and money.

Online Shopping

The "dot.com" boom of a few years ago saw the rapid rise and equally rapid fall of numerous companies selling goods and services on the Internet. While many companies disappeared, lots of others have developed successful online businesses. These provide a very quick and easy method of purchasing goods without the need to travel to the shops. Of course, we are really talking about *online ordering*, since someone still has to physically collect the goods from a warehouse and deliver them to our door.

One of the first major online stores was **Amazon.com** of America and **Amazon.co.uk** in the United Kingdom.

Originally known for selling mainly books, Amazon has now extended its range to include many other products such as music and video, toys, home and garden and electronic goods such as cameras and computer equipment.

Initially you must set up an account with a password, your name and address and e-mail address.

After logging onto the Amazon site (which you might have placed in your list of **Favorites** or **Bookmarks** for convenience), you browse the categories. For example in the music category there are links down the left-hand side for the different types of music such as **Classical, Jazz, Pop** and **Easy Listening**.

Please note that Amazon also provides a **Marketplace** where you can buy and sell your own items, with access to a market of millions of people. It differs from the online auction sites such as eBay since there is no bidding process – the prices are fixed by the seller.

When you have found an item of interest, such as a book or
CD, there is usually a link to click for more details. In the
case of a book this may be the author's synopsis of the
contents and customers' reviews of the product. In the case
of a music CD the further details would be a list of all of
the tracks.

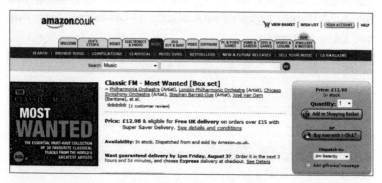

If you intend to buy more than one item, select **Add to
Shopping Basket** as shown on the right above. Then further
items can be selected and added to the basket. If you only
want a single item, it can be bought immediately with *one
click* as shown above right as ***Buy Now with 1-Click***. For this
latter option you must have already set up an account with
your credit card details, your name and address and e-mail
address. Then the whole transaction can be completed with
no further input from you.

When you finish adding items to your shopping basket you
need to click **Proceed to Checkout** to pay for the goods by
credit card and give address and credit card details if you
are a new customer. You will be informed by e-mail of the
progress of your order and when it has been dispatched.

As well as buying music CDs by mail order, millions of
music tracks are now available for purchase by
downloading over the Internet, as discussed shortly.

Supermarket Shopping Online

In principle, the home shopping schemes operated by firms like Tesco and Sainsbury are similar to Amazon. Again your credit card details must be provided. At the core of your order is your basic shopping list of items bought regularly, every week, say. Items can be added to the list or removed. Any item which is not in stock may be substituted by the staff with an equivalent item, perhaps of a different brand. Or you can choose not to have substitutions for out-of-stock items.

Delivery charges are typically in the range £4 – £6 depending on the time slot, which you select from a grid of available times. Against this must be considered the saving in your time and transport costs. Ordering a weekly shop online only takes a few minutes compared with at least an hour or two for a trip to the supermarket – not to mention the stress and effort when the store's really busy.

Tracing Your Family History

In later life many of us enjoy finding out about our ancestors. While some of this research still involves traditional methods such as visiting local record offices and churchyards and contacting relatives, the Internet is an incredibly powerful tool for this work. A great deal of work has been done to make census and parish records available online; so you can find a huge amount of information about your forebears without even leaving home.

A good way to start is to type the keyword **genealogy** into a search engine; you should find a host of relevant Web sites.

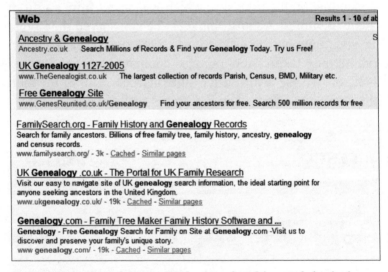

Some of the best known Web sites for this work include:

www.ancestry.co.uk	**www.familysearch.org**
www.genuki.org.uk	**www.1901censusonline.com**
www.familytreemaker.com	**www.pro.gov.uk**
www.familyrecords.gov.uk	**www.genesreunited.co.uk**

Many of these sites give access to large databases of family records, births, deaths, marriages, etc., together with general advice on researching your family using both the Internet and traditional methods. Some sites also contain the names of specialist researchers who, for a fee, will undertake some of the work for you.

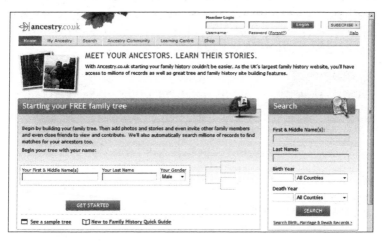

The site **www.findmypast.com**, (formerly known as **www.1837online.org**) provides listings of births, marriages and deaths from 1837 – 2005. Then, from the reference numbers provided, you can complete an online order form for copies of actual birth, marriage and death certificates to be sent to you by the traditional postal service.

The GENUKI Web site is maintained by a charitable organization and provides data bases of parish and other records for the United Kingdom and Ireland. Advice for newcomers to genealogy is also given.

Some of the genealogy Web sites listed earlier include help and software to compile your own family Web site. Such a site has been created in my own family by Mark Gatenby (**www.gatenby.freeserve.co.uk**) and attracts a large number of visitors making contributions from around the world. There are several different aspects to Mark's site. First there is a family forum which allows you to post messages asking for information about particular relatives. These are available for viewing worldwide.

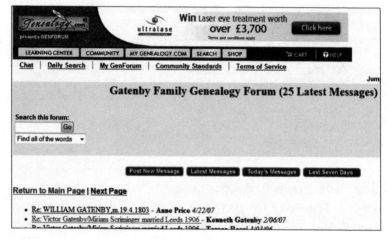

All being well a request for information will result in lots of replies, like the one shown below.

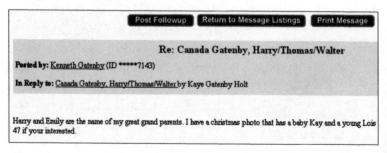

Across the top of Mark's site is a menu bar giving access to family records from around the United Kingdom. The various menus include **Births, Marriages**, various **Censuses**, **Places** and **Family Trees**.

Address	http://www.gatenby.freeserve.co.uk/					
Births	Marriages	Census	Places	Parish Rcds	Family Trees	Main page

		Ga	Clton Miniott	Whitby		
Gatenby	**Date**		Aldborough	**Spouse**	**Age**	**Notes**
ann	30 September 1795	ri	Kirby Wiske	ra	9m	father carpenter
ann	16 November 1809	th	Ripon	th	2	
ann	22 May 1822		Well		65	
ann	06 October 1833		Whitby		59	
barbara	06 September 1833		Scotland	Deaths	0	
dinah	07 June 1787			john	82	wid john carpenter –
elizabeth	15 April 1763			william		van carpenter
elizabeth	20 April 1770	ann & late joseph			34	father sailor

The family tree for my own branch of the family is found under the **Overseas** menu, reflecting the exodus of families from Yorkshire to Canada in the last century.

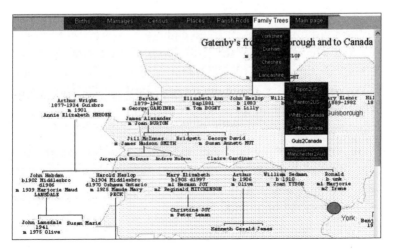

The 1901 Census Online

This site (**www.1901censusonline.com**) is provided by The National Archives (formerly known as The Public Record Office). The entire records for the 1901 Census for England and Wales have been placed on the Internet, including copies of the original handwritten enumerators' forms. The site was initially overwhelmed with users and facilities had to be greatly increased. You can search using several criteria such as a person's name, gender, date of birth and place of birth.

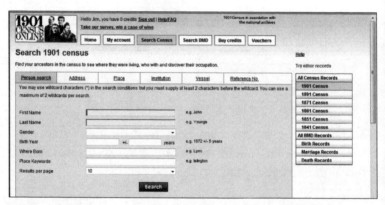

If the search is successful you can open an Account Session with a charge of £5 for 500 credits. You can check in advance the cost of different pieces of information. Payment may be made by credit card or by the use of vouchers bought in advance from suppliers such as public libraries.

With certain browsers, you can view and print an image of the original handwritten document listing details of every member of a household. Alternatively you can order a copy of the image to be posted to you.

As shown below, you can print out a transcript of the census form for a household, listing all of the members including name, sex, age, occupation, where born and relationship to the head of the family.

Person Details

Full Transcription Details for **Mary Gatenby** <u>View Image/Other Household members</u>

PRO Reference			
RG Number, Series	Piece	Folio	Page
RG13	4577	78	8

Name		
Mary Gatenby		
Relation to Head of Family	Condition as to Marriage	Age Last Birthday
Head	W	45
Profession or Occupation	Employment Status	
	Undefined	
Where Born	Address	
Yorkshire Kildale	10 Borough Rd West	
Civil Parish	Rural District	
Middlesbro		
Town or Village or Hamlet	Parliamentary Borough or Division	
Middlesbrough	Middlesbro	

The 1901 Census Web Site is available 24 hours a day, 7 days a week.

Originally only the 1901 census data was available online, but in recent years census data has been added for 1841, 1851, 1861, 1871, 1891.

Downloading Music

A few years ago you could download *free* music tracks to your computer by making copies over the Internet from other computers containing the required tracks. After some legal battles many companies now *sell* legal copies of music by downloading the files over the Internet to your computer. So if you hear a piece of music you like, you can download and save a copy straightaway, without waiting for delivery by post or visiting a music shop. You can even play a sample online to make sure it's the right track.

There are several formats for audio files saved on disc, such as *Windows Media Audio (WMA)* and *MP3*. Once you've downloaded an album or perhaps just a single track, you can play it on your computer in Windows Media Player 11, provided as part of Windows Vista. Alternatively the downloaded music can be "burned" to a standard audio CD or copied to a portable MP3 player or similar and some mobile phones.

Sites providing music can be found by entering keywords like **music downloads** in a search engine such as Google. Two of the most popular sites are iTunes and Napster.

Tesco.com has a **Music Downloads** link in the **Entertainments & Books** section of its main shopping web site. After clicking the link you are presented with the main music download page shown below.

You can find music by entering, into the search bar at the top of the screen, words from the title or the artist's name. Or you can browse through the various categories, genres, artists A-Z, etc., down the left-hand side of the download screen shown above. Some of the sites have millions of records to choose from. Once you've found the music you want, prices are given for albums and individual tracks as shown on the next page.

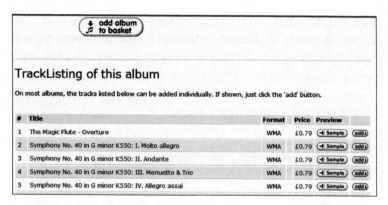

At the time of writing albums cost around £7.99 and individual tracks are 79 pence. If you're not sure what each track sounds like there's a **Sample** button which allows you to play a short excerpt. To buy a track, or an album, click the **add** button to place it in your basket.

The first time you download music you need to register by entering your e-mail address and a password; for subsequent music purchases you sign in as an existing user. Next select **go to checkout** and **confirm my order**, before entering your personal details including your credit card and security code. Once your credit card details have been accepted click the **Download** button, then **Save** on the **File Download** window shown below.

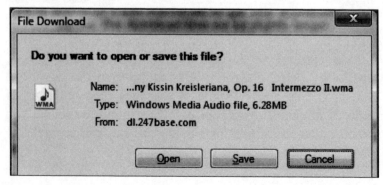

You are presented with the **Save As** dialogue box as shown below. If you wish you can accept the default **File name** and folder (**Jim\Downloads** in this example) for the saved file; or you can provide your own **File name** and save location.

Click **Save** again and the download begins. If you are using broadband, the message **Download Complete** is soon displayed in the progress window and you are given the chance to **Open** and play the downloaded music in the Windows Media Player.

In this example, a Windows Media Audio file was saved in the folder **C: Users\Jim\Downloads**. If you open this folder in the Windows Vista Computer/Explorer feature you can see the music file. Allow the cursor to hover over the file name or icon to see the file details, as shown below.

Double-click the icon to launch Windows Media Player 11 and play the track. It can then be added to your music library and playlists in the Windows Media Player.

Windows Media Player 11 is provided as part of Windows Vista. It is described in more detail in our companion book "Computing with Vista for the Older Generation" from Bernard Babani (publishing) Ltd.

If you right-click over the icon for the track in the Vista Computer/Explorer feature as shown on page 167, a menu appears allowing you to select **Send To** in order to copy the track to a CD/DVD or a portable device connected to your computer. These devices will appear in the **Send To** menu shown below, for example **Removable Disk (G:)**.

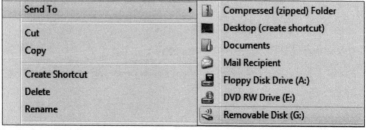

Downloading Software

Fast *broadband* connections make it feasible to download large files from the Internet to your computer, as discussed in the previous section on downloading music. In contrast *dial-up* connections are very slow when downloading large files. As well as music and video, *software* is often supplied as a download rather than as a boxed package. Instruction manuals can be included in the download as PDF (Portable Document Format) files, to be read using the Adobe Reader program, itself available as a free download.

Device drivers are pieces of software which enable equipment such as printers and graphics cards to work with the Windows Vista operating system. For example, when Windows Vista first came out, it was necessary to obtain new Vista drivers for certain older models of printer. These are usually available free as downloads from the printer manufacturer's Web site, unless the device is no longer supported. Files to be downloaded are normally saved in a compressed format to speed up the process. Therefore, after downloading, the files need to be expanded again before they can be installed or set up.

The general download method is as follows:

- Log on to the manufacturer's Web site.
- Locate the correct driver or piece of software.
- Click the **Download** button.
- Click the **Save** button.
- Choose a folder or accept the default **Save** folder.
- Wait as the software is downloaded.
- Click **Run** to expand the compressed download file.
- Finally, install the new software or device driver.

You are told when the download is complete.

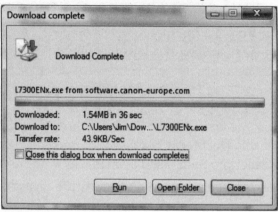

It is then necessary to expand the downloaded file, usually by clicking **Run** as shown above and then **Unzip** in the **WinZip Self-Extractor** shown below.

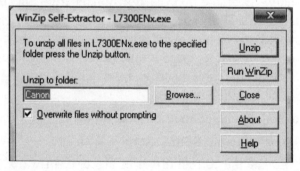

The software or device driver must now be installed or set up; this process may start automatically or you may need to double-click on a **Setup** file in the folder where you saved the **Unzipped** folder, such as the **Canon** folder above. In the case of driver software, you may be asked to connect the hardware first and then, when requested, give the folder location on your hard disc where you saved the driver.

Internet Banking and Security

Introduction

It's now possible to carry out many of your banking activities from home. There's no longer any need to travel to a branch unless a face-to-face meeting is absolutely necessary or you need to withdraw actual cash.

Obviously many people will be concerned about security, but reputable banks and financial institutions guarantee that in the event of fraud, customers won't lose any money. Internet security is discussed in more detail later, but one of the main security methods is to *encrypt* (or encode) all information sent between your computer and the bank's. However, serious criminals are now targeting the Internet and finding ways to beating the system with frauds like "phishing" and software which detects the keys you press.

Viruses, worms and Trojans are known as *malware*, short for malicious software. These are small computer programs designed to cause damage and inconvenience to computer users. A great deal of security software is now available and this is discussed in the second half of this chapter, together with commonsense precautions which should help to safeguard your money and personal data.

10 Internet Banking and Security

To participate in *online banking*, you need a computer and modem and an account with an Internet Service Provider. To find out more about online banking, log on to the Web sites of any of the major banks, such as the Halifax, at **www.halifax.co.uk** and the Bank of Scotland, at **www.bankofscotland.co.uk**.

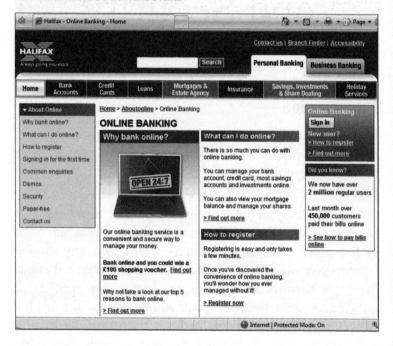

With online banking you can see at a glance the various accounts available from a particular bank and also make comparisons with other online banks. Internet savings accounts usually pay a better rate of interest than the traditional account based on a pass book – after all, you do much of the work previously done by cashiers while sitting at your computer.

The bank Web site should provide lots of information and on-screen demos of the range of services offered. A major advantage of online banking is that you can access your accounts at almost *any time of the day or night* – there's no need to wait for normal banking hours.

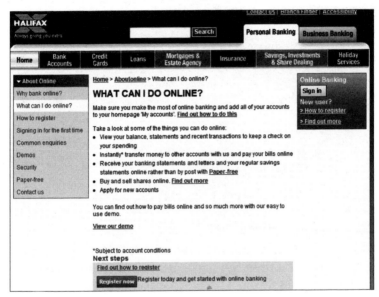

With online banking you will be able to carry out many of the normal banking functions, such as:

- View your balance
- Print a statement
- Pay bills including proof of payment and date
- Transfer funds between your various accounts
- Transfer money to another person's account
- Set up standing orders
- Apply for an increased overdraft
- Check and cancel direct debits.

There should also be a link to initiate the opening of an online bank account. The Web sites for the Halifax and Bank of Scotland both have links leading to demonstrations which give you a tour of the online banking service. The following extract shows a sample of the online Bank Account Statement from the Halifax.

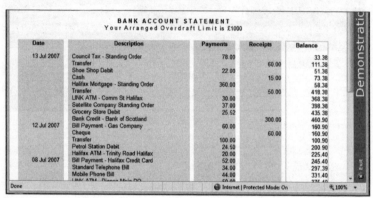

Once you have signed up for online banking, your bank will arrange with you a *username* (sometimes also called a *login name* or a *user ID*) and a *password*. Shown below is the login screen for the Halifax Online Service.

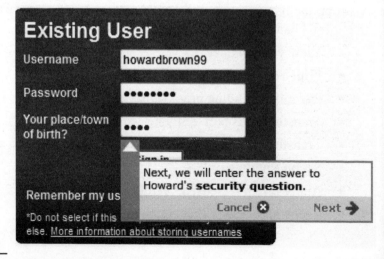

You may be asked to provide at least one additional piece of security information, such as a parent's name, some memorable piece of personal information or a secret question and answer. If you forget your password there is usually a number to ring to arrange a new one. This is when you need to know the additional security information to prove your identity. Obviously all security information such as passwords, etc., should be kept safe and not written down and left in obvious places.

Once you have opened an online bank account you can view your list of accounts. This gives an overview of your various accounts with the bank, allowing you to make transfers and pay bills, etc.

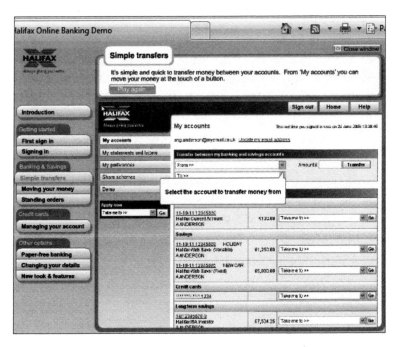

Secure Transactions

Carrying out financial transactions over the Internet is bound to be a cause for concern. Online banking involves sending and receiving personal financial information between your computer and that of the bank. Internet shopping and paying for goods online, as discussed in the last chapter, requires us to give our credit card details to suppliers. One estimate put the annual cost to British banks of online fraud at £33.5 million in 2006.

There are many simple precautions which individuals can take to make fraud difficult. For example, when making online purchases, use a credit card with a low limit – then you can't lose very much.

Passwords

As well as a *username*, you will be issued with or choose your own *password*. This should not be obvious like the name of a pet or family member. Your password doesn't appear on the screen (usually replaced by a line of dots), but beware of anyone looking over your shoulder.

- Never leave your password lying around, in fact don't write it down at all.

- Don't walk away and leave the computer open at your bank account. Some systems log you out if the computer is not used for 10 minutes

- Always *log out* or *sign off* when you have finished using the computer.

- Don't give anyone your username or password.

- Change your password regularly.

- Computers in public places may not be secure – don't use them for important financial transactions.

Secure Servers

Servers are the computers used by banks and other large organizations to hold the details of millions of transactions and customers' accounts. *Secure servers* use *encryption* to prevent criminals from accessing financial or confidential information sent between computers. Encryption scrambles or encodes the information so that it can only be decoded or made intelligible by authorized users.

Whenever you are online to a secure server, a small closed padlock icon appears on your screen. Double-click the padlock icon to reveal details of the security certificate issued to the company. Always deal with companies who use secure servers.

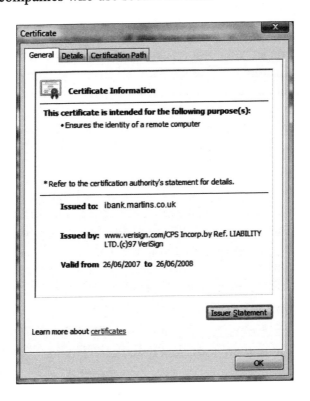

The Dangers

If you take no action to improve your computer's security, here are some of the threats which might attack the system.

Malware

A virus, worm, Trojan horse or spyware, etc., can cause damage to your data or collect information for criminal purposes. The Trojan is a program which appears to be genuine but actually contains malicious code; for example to give someone a "backdoor" into your computer.

Hackers

Malicious computer users may connect to your computer and steal your files and personal information.

Spyware

A piece of software can be installed on your computer which tracks your key presses and sends the information back to criminals. The spyware might be delivered to your computer during the downloading of some apparently genuine free software. Always save downloaded software first and run it through an anti-virus/Internet security program like F-Secure or Norton 360 before installing it.

Phishing

A genuine-looking e-mail may appear to be from your bank and ask you to update your personal information. Sometimes the e-mail asks you to click a link to another Web site set up by the fraudsters. Banks never ask you to input your personal information by e-mail. Don't open e-mails unless you are sure the sender is genuine.

Spam or Junk Mail

Unsolicited e-mails clog up your inbox and might even cause you to miss important messages.

Protecting Your Computer

The Windows Security Center in Windows Vista contains a number of software features to protect your computer against the sort of dangers listed on the previous page. The **Security Center** is started from icons in the **Security Center**

Control Panel in **Classic View** and **Home View**. It allows you to make sure the **Windows Firewall** and **Windows Defender** are switched on to guard against spyware and other attempts to attack you computer. The Security Center also works with any third-party security software such as Norton AntiVirus and F-Secure Internet Security and makes sure they are switched on and up to date.

Switching on **Automatic updating** ensures that the latest security software developments for Windows Vista are downloaded and installed on your computer.

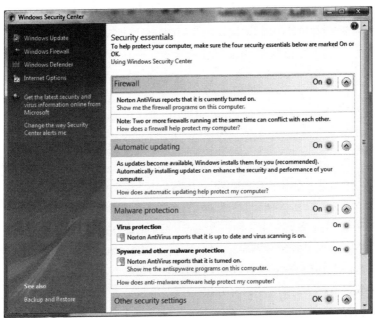

Internet Explorer 7, which is part of Windows Vista, provides its own **Phishing Filter**, and **Pop-Up Blocker** on the **Tools** menu. At the bottom of the screen there is an option to turn **Protected Mode On** or **Off**. **Protected Mode** is intended to stop malicious software being installed. These topics are discussed on pages 127 – 129 of this book.

Windows Vista doesn't contain its own anti-virus software so it's a good idea to install one of the many popular packages such as Norton 360 from Symantec or F-Secure Internet Security. As well as protecting against viruses, these two packages are also intended to guard against spyware, hackers and spam. There are many thousands of computer viruses and malware and new ones are constantly being invented. Packages like Norton 360 and F-Secure provide regular automatic updates enabling the latest viruses to be detected and removed from the computer.

Security software should provide the following safeguards:

- Detect and destroy all viruses, worms and malware.
- Enable both manual and scheduled scans of all disc drives, etc.
- Scan all incoming e-mails, attachments and software downloaded from the Internet.
- Include a firewall to protect against hackers.
- Include protection against spyware.
- Provide automatic updates of virus definitions.
- Keep your computer free from spam e-mails.
- Enable parents (and grandparents) to control children's access to Web sites and limit "surfing" time to a reasonable amount.

Using E-mail

Introduction

E-mail is one of the most popular uses of the Internet. It enables people to communicate rapidly with friends, relatives and colleagues around the world. E-mail has several important advantages over the ordinary post and the telephone, for example:

- An e-mail travels to its destination almost instantly. If the intended recipient is online they can get your message immediately.

- The same e-mail can be sent to several different people by simply clicking their names in an electronic address book.

- An e-mail can be sent at any time – day or night.

- You don't have to make direct contact with the other person – if they're out of their home they will see your message next time they read their mail.

- You can send *attachments* with e-mails. These can be photographs, sound or video clips or document files containing text and pictures, for example.

- E-mails can be saved and printed out on paper.

However, there are some negative aspects to e-mail, which can cause some people a great deal of stress:

- People at work may be inundated by e-mails, many of them trivial and unnecessary.

- "Spam" or unsolicited junk mail may annoy you and clog your Inbox.

- "Phishing" e-mails attempt to trick the recipient into revealing their financial details.

- An e-mail may spread a virus which can damage the files on your hard disc.

- Some e-mails tend to be written in a hurry, perhaps with less emphasis on style, content and grammar, possibly causing a decline in traditional letter writing skills.

In spite of these potential problems, e-mail seems likely to remain a major method of communication, especially where speed is important.

Introducing Windows Mail

This is a new e-mail program introduced as part of Windows Vista; it is known as an *e-mail client* and replaces Outlook Express provided in earlier versions of Windows.

You can launch **Windows Mail** from the **Start** menu in Vista or from the **Start**, **All Programs** menu.

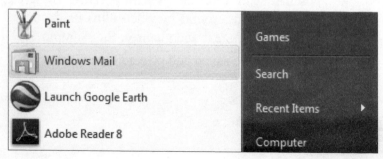

Your computer may already have on icon for Windows Mail on the Vista Desktop, as shown on the right. If not you can create an icon by right-clicking **Windows Mail** in the **Start** or **All Programs** menu, then selecting **Send To** and clicking **Desktop (create shortcut)**. Double-click this icon to launch Windows Mail.

The first time you try to send an e-mail, you need to enter some details for your e-mail account. These are provided by your Internet Service Provider such as BT, etc. Your information should be of a similar format to the examples listed on the right below.

	Example
E-mail address:	**johnsmith@btinternet.com**
Username:	**johnsmith**
Password:	********
POP3 Incoming mail server:	**mail.btinternet.com**
SMTP Outgoing mail server:	**mail.btinternet.com**

Mail servers listed above are the computers that handle the mail at your Internet Service Provider's premises.

POP3 above stands for Post Office Protocol 3 and is frequently used for personal e-mails. This type of server holds your incoming messages until you read your e-mail – then they are downloaded to your computer.

SMTP above stands for Simple Mail Transfer Protocol. This server sends your outgoing e-mails to their destinations on the Internet.

Setting Up an E-mail Account in Windows Mail

The first time you try to use Windows Mail, the setup wizard starts up and a dialogue box, shown below, requires you to enter your **Display name** as you would like it to appear in the **From** field on the messages you send.

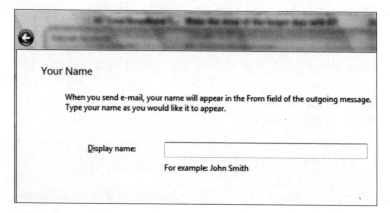

Click **Next** and the dialogue box shown below appears. Here you enter your unique, personal e-mail address, given to you by your Internet Service Provider.

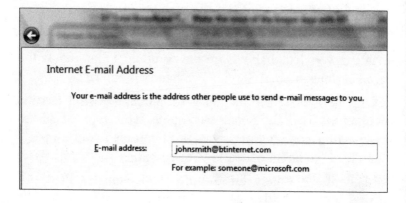

After clicking **Next** again you are required to set up your e-mail servers, as shown below.

Set up e-mail servers

> Incoming e-mail server type:
>
> POP3 ▼
>
> Incoming mail (POP3 or IMAP) server:
>
> Outgoing e-mail server (SMTP) name:
>
> ☐ Outgoing server requires authentication
>
> Where can I find my e-mail server information?

Many home users connect to **POP3** incoming mail servers, as mentioned earlier. If not, click the down arrow to the right of **POP3** shown above; this displays the small menu shown on the right.

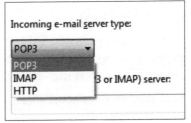

IMAP on the menu on the right stands for Internet Message Access Protocol. These incoming mail servers, widely used in business, don't download your e-mails to your computer but instead allow you to view and manage the messages while they are still on the server. Select **IMAP** if your ISP uses this type of incoming mail server. **HTTP** above refers to Web-based e-mail such as Hotmail, but this type of server is not compatible with Windows Mail.

Now enter the names of your incoming and outgoing e-mail servers, as provided by your ISP. These should be of a similar format to the examples shown on page 183.

Also click the check box as shown on the previous page so that a tick appears next to **Outgoing server requires authentication**.

Finally enter the **E-mail username** and **Password** provided by your Internet Service Provider and, if you wish, tick the box next to **Remember password**.

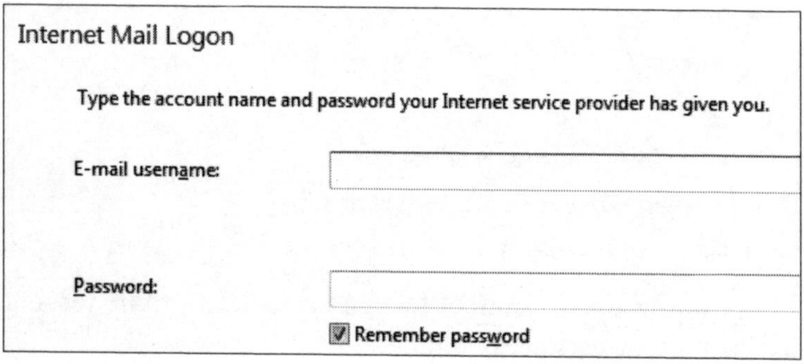

Internet Mail Logon

Type the account name and password your Internet service provider has given you.

E-mail username:

Password:

☑ Remember password

On clicking **Next** you are congratulated on setting up your new e-mail account. You can now go back to Windows Mail, read any welcoming messages in your **Inbox** and start creating your first message as described shortly.

Setting Up Further E-mail Accounts

You may wish to set up further e-mail accounts on your computer, either for yourself or other members of your family. From the Windows Mail **Inbox**, select **Tools**, **Accounts...**, **Mail**, **Add...**, **E-mail Account** and click **Next**. The Internet Account Wizard opens up with the **Your Name** dialogue box displayed. The new account can now be set up as before, completing each dialogue and clicking **Next** as just described from page 184 onwards.

E-mail Addresses

In order to send someone an e-mail message you must know their unique e-mail address. This may appear on their ordinary correspondence, business card, etc., and will also be displayed on any e-mails they send you.

When you sign up for an Internet account you will be able to choose, or be given, your own e-mail address. This is a unique location enabling your mail to reach you from anywhere in the world.

Common types of e-mail address are as follows:

stella@aol.com
james@msn.com
enquiries@wildlife.org.uk

The part of the e-mail address in front of the **@** sign is normally your Internet *username* or *login* name. The second part of the address identifies the mail server computer at your company, organization or Internet Service Provider. The last part of the address is the type of organisation providing the service. In the previous addresses, **.com** refers to a commercial company. Other organisation types include:

.org	non-profit making organisations
.co	UK commercial company
.net	Internet company
.biz	business
.me.uk	UK individual
.co.uk	UK business

A two-digit country code such as **uk** or **fr** may be added to the end of the e-mail address.

Using Windows Mail

Launch Windows Mail from the **Start** or **All Programs** menu or by double-clicking its icon on the Desktop. The first screen you see is the Windows Mail **Inbox**.

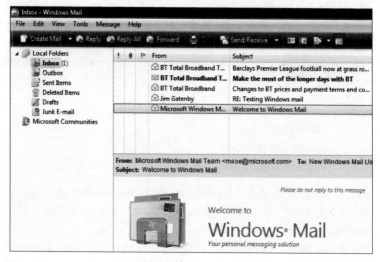

There may already be one or two incoming messages listed under **From**, **Subject**, etc., such as **Welcome to Windows Mail** shown above. Notice that if you select an incoming e-mail in the list, the contents of the message are displayed on the screen in the area below. The **Welcome** example above shows that e-mails are not limited to plain text but can use various text fonts and also include pictures.

Down the left-hand side of the **Inbox** screen above are the folders for storing messages. Apart from the **Inbox**, the **Outbox** contains messages waiting to be sent, after which they are listed in the **Sent Items** folder. You can delete old e-mails, placing them in the **Deleted Items** folder. Any e-mails which the program decides are "spam" or unsolicited advertising, etc., go in the **Junk E-mail** folder.

Creating an E-mail Message

From the **Inbox** screen select **Create Mail**, as shown below.

The new message window opens and you may wish to click the **Maximise** button shown on the right (in the middle) if you are sending a lengthy message.

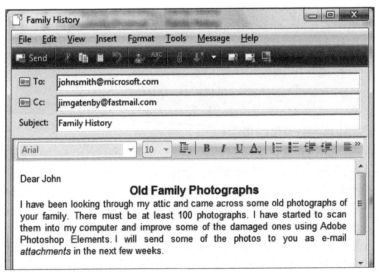

In the **To:** field enter the e-mail address of the person who is to receive the message. You can send messages to more than one person, using semi-colons to separate their addresses. In the **Cc:** field shown above enter the e-mail addresses of anyone who is to receive a "carbon" copy. Next enter a meaningful heading in the **Subject** field.

You are now ready to start entering the text of the message.

Entering the main body text for your message is very similar to using a simple word processor. You can change the font or style of lettering and use effects such as bold, underline, colour, bullets and numbering. You can also use editing features such as "cut and paste".

Inserting a Picture Within the Text of a Message

A picture can be embedded in an e-mail by clicking **Insert** shown below, then selecting **Picture...** and browsing to find and select the picture from your hard disc. The picture becomes part of the text of the message, unlike the *attachment* discussed below.

Adding an Attachment

You can attach files from your hard disc to an e-mail. Attachments are often photographs or word processing and spreadsheet documents. Anyone receiving the attachment can download the file and open it separately on their computer. To attach a file such as a photograph to an e-mail, click the paperclip **Attach** icon on the Windows Mail Toolbar shown below.

Next the Computer/Explorer feature opens, allowing you to locate and select the required picture or document from your computer. When you click the **Open** button, the file is attached to the e-mail as shown below in the **Attach** field. If necessary you can send more than one attachment.

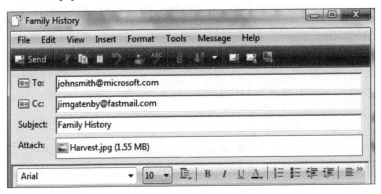

Once the text has been entered and any attachments added, click the **Send** button to get your message on its way.

Receiving an E-mail

When you want to check your mail, open your **Inbox** and click **Send/Receive** as shown below. Extra **Send and Receive** options are also available from the **Tools** menu shown above and below. As a test, I sent the previously described e-mail, **Family History**, to my own e-mail address.

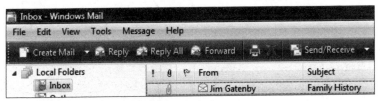

As shown, the **Family History** message is in my **Inbox**; the attached photo is denoted by a paper clip icon.

Double-click on the entry for the e-mail as listed in the **Inbox** on the previous page. The message opens for you to read, in its own window as shown below.

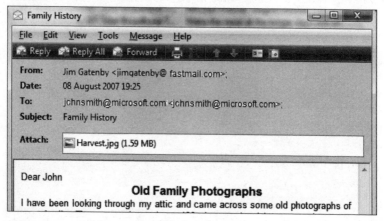

You can reply to the originator after clicking **Reply** or **Reply All** (to include all of the original recipients). The addresses of the reply recipients and the subject are automatically filled in – just add your message to the top of the original message. There is also an icon in the middle of the Toolbar to print out the e-mail, as shown below right.

Double-clicking the entry in the **Attach** field shown above opens the photo or document in its associated program, e.g. the Windows Photo Gallery or Word, where it can be edited, etc., and saved on your hard  disc. Or click the file in the messages list and then select **File** and **Save Attachments...** from the toolbar.

Avoiding Junk Mail or "Spam"

Many companies and individuals send out unsolicited e-mails advertising a product or service or possibly trying to trick you into parting with money. At the very least these can be a nuisance. The junk e-mail filter catches the obvious spam messages and transfers them straight to a special **Junk E-mail** folder away from your **Inbox**. You can adjust the amount of junk e-mail protection you receive by altering the settings in the **Junk E-mails Options** dialogue box shown below. From the **Inbox** select **Tools** and **Junk E-mail Options...**.

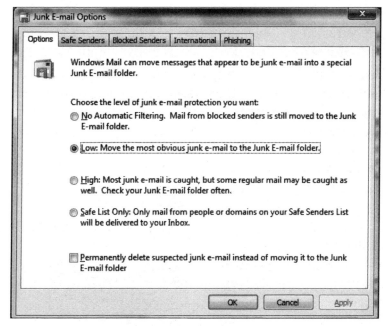

The **Junk E-mail** folder in the **Inbox** has a **Message** menu which allows you to **Mark as Not Junk...** a selected message. Senders or domains can be added to a **Safe Senders** list or a **Blocked Senders** list.

E-mail Etiquette or Netiquette

An e-mail message can be sent with a single click of a button and reach its destination anywhere in the world in a matter of seconds or minutes. A hasty e-mail can do a lot of damage in no time at all – there's no time for a "cooling off" period. Similarly it's not a good idea to dash off a hasty message late at night, especially if you've had a nightcap or two.

E-mails tend to be written very quickly and perhaps with less care than the conventional hand-written or typed letter. An e-mail can be forwarded to lots of other people in seconds or minutes; some people have been severely embarrassed and even lost their jobs through irresponsible forwarding of e-mails containing sensitive information.

Messages written entirely in capital letters are seen as offensive by some people and are known as "yelling". An e-mail may not convey emotions very well and jokes may be misunderstood. A set of *emoticons* has been designed, each made up of two or three keyboard characters and intended to express the tone of an e-mail more clearly.

:) or :-)	Smiling, happy, joking
:(or :-(	Frowning or unhappy
:-|	Indifferent
:-o	Surprised
:-x	Not saying anything
:-p	Sticking out your tongue
:-D	Laughing

A more comprehensive list of emoticons for use in e-mails is provided by SmileyWorld, Ltd at the Web site:

www.windweaver.com/emoticon.htm

Newsgroups

This is a feature in Windows mail which allows you to have a discussion on a topic in which you are interested. Start Windows Mail and click **Newsgroups...** on the **Tools** menu on the **Inbox** toolbar. The first time you open **Newsgroups** you have to wait a short time while the long list of available newsgroups is compiled. Scroll down the list and if you want to investigate a group, select the group and then click the **Go to** button at the bottom of the **Newsgroup Subscriptions** window shown below.

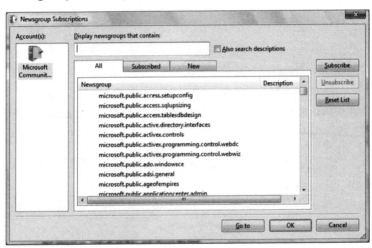

If you want to join in a newsgroup, click the **Subscribe** button shown on the right above. Then you can access the newsgroup quickly by clicking on it in the **Microsoft Communities** folder of your Windows Mail **Inbox**, as shown on the right. To open the newsgroup, click its entry under **Microsoft Communities**.

The newsgroup opens as shown below.

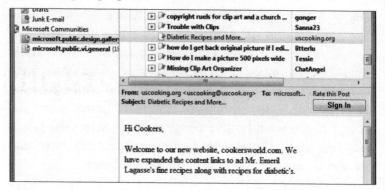

To view the text of a message, click on its entry in the list shown above in the example **Diabetic Recipes and More....**

Posting a Newsgroup Message

To write a newsgroup posting, click the **Write Message** icon shown on the right, on the left of the Windows Mail toolbar.

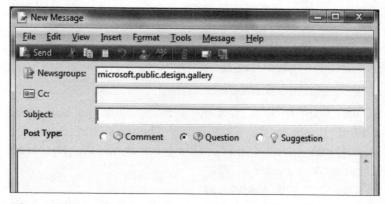

The **Subject** of the message and the main text are now entered just like an e-mail; the main difference is that the message is sent to an entire group of subscribers to a newsgroup – not just to one or more e-mail contacts.

Preparing and Sending Photographs

Introduction

There are many occasions when it's useful to be able to send photographs over the Internet; a common method is to send them as e-mail attachments, as discussed in the last chapter. A major use of photographs on the Internet is the exchange of pictures between friends and family. However, there are many other practical applications, such as sending an image of a medical condition or injury to a specialist in another part of the world, for example.

Digital photographs occupy a great deal of space when saved on a disc and also when transferred around the Internet. This can make images slow to download to a computer and open on the screen – very frustrating for the e-mail recipient or "surfer". Digital cameras normally save images as JPEG files, an abbreviation for Joint Photographic Experts Group. This is a method of "compressing" image files by discarding unnecessary detail, without losing too much quality. JPEG files use less disc space and can be transferred quickly over the Internet.

While JPEG is popular for sending photographs, another format, TIFF (Tagged Image File Format), is used for high quality glossy photographic prints. However, TIFF files are extremely large and bulky for sending over the Internet.

Shown above is a JPEG photograph saved on a hard disc and displayed in the Windows Explorer/Computer feature. You can see that even as a JPEG compressed file, the image occupies a hefty 1.34MB and uses 2816x2112 *pixels*, the tiny picture elements used to make up the image. As discussed shortly, various methods are used for transferring digital images onto a computer and these generally use the JPEG compressed format. To reduce the size of a JPEG file further it may be necessary to reduce the actual area of the image, using cropping as discussed shortly. Alternatively you can change the resolution, in pixels, at the expense of a loss in image quality.

Saving Images in Different File Formats

Images may be opened in the Windows Paint program and saved in various file formats, such as JPEG, TIFF and GIF, using the **File** and **Save As...** option, as shown on the right.

File name:	Alcazaba
Save as type:	TIFF (*.tif;*.tiff)

de Folders	Monochrome Bitmap (*.bmp;*.dib)
	16 Color Bitmap (*.bmp;*.dib)
	256 Color Bitmap (*.bmp;*.dib)
	24-bit Bitmap (*.bmp;*.dib)
	JPEG (*.jpg;*.jpeg;*.jpe;*.jfif)
	GIF (*.gif)
	TIFF (*.tif;*.tiff)
	PNG (*.png)

JPEG Compressed Image Files

The JPEG file uses what is known as *lossy* compression; it works by discarding some of the detail, colour, etc., from the pixels in an image. This reduces the image size and speeds up transfer times on the Internet and in e-mail attachments. The original full size image contains a lot of detail not visible to the human eye. This superfluous detail can be safely removed in the compression process without seriously affecting the appearance. Digital editing programs like Adobe Photoshop Elements shown below allow you to set the amount of compression when saving a JPEG file.

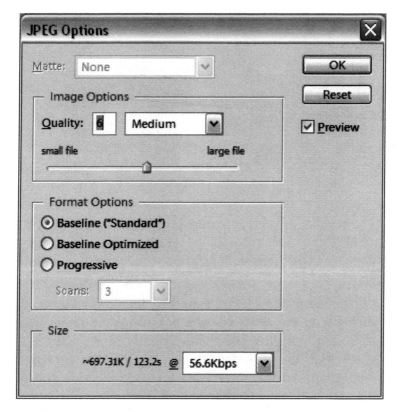

In the **JPEG Options** dialogue box shown on the previous page, you can move a slider (shown below) to vary the amount of compression. The slider ranges between **small file, low quality** to **large file, high quality**.

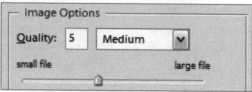

The image below was saved first as **high quality,** with the slider in the **large file** position. Then the original file was saved again as a **small file, low quality** as shown below right. As far as I could see there was no obvious difference in quality of the two images displayed on the screen.

The number of pixels remained the same in both images at 1600x1200, but the amount of detail in the pixels is different. The high quality file was approximately 10 times the size of the low quality file (1057.31K versus 101.91K).

Adobe Photoshop Elements displays the download time for each file in the **JPEG Options** box shown on the previous page; the large file had a download time of 10 times the small file. The download times for 2MB/sec broadband were approximately 35 times faster than for a 56K modem.

Sources of Digital Photographs

There are several ways of acquiring images to be saved on your computer then sent as e-mail attachments or uploaded to a Web site. These include:

The Digital Camera

In the digital camera, images are stored on a memory card, readable by a computer and capable of storing hundreds of photographs. The camera is normally supplied with a USB cable, for connecting it to a computer.

The cable from the camera plugs into one of the computer's USB ports; these are usually located on the front or back of the main base unit of the computer.

USB Ports

Windows Vista contains the necessary software to import digital photographs from a digital camera and save them in a folder on your hard disc. As discussed shortly, the Windows Photo Gallery can be used to import, manage, display, edit and e-mail digital photographs.

The Memory Card Reader

You can take the memory card out of your camera and place it into a separate card reader. There are several types of memory card and the readers are capable of accommodating the different sizes and shapes. Some card readers are stand-alone devices which plug straight into a USB port. Others may be part of a multi-function printer which can also act as a scanner and photocopier.

The Scanner

You may have some very old photographic prints which you want to add to your computer archive or share with someone by e-mail. The flatbed scanner

plugs into a USB port and allows you to copy old photographs and store them as digital images on your hard disc. Then you can improve them in the Windows Photo Gallery. Digital editing software such as Corel Paint Shop Pro or Adobe Photoshop Elements allows you to polish up an old image, for example by removing scratches or editing out unwanted objects or even people.

Some of the latest multi-function printers incorporate a built-in flat-bed scanner.

The Bluetooth Mobile Phone

Bluetooth is a technology which allows you to connect devices such as mobile phones to your computer, without the use of cables. In addition to mobile phones, Bluetooth can be used to connect wirelessly devices like printers, mice, keyboards and headsets.

All you need to capture and transfer images to a computer is a "Bluetooth enabled" camera phone and a Bluetooth USB adapter in the form of a USB dongle, as shown on the right. Make sure the dongle is  compatible with Windows Vista. The dongle package includes a Bluetooth software CD.

With the dongle inserted in a USB port, the computer can detect any mobile phone within range. When detected an icon for the phone appears in the Bluetooth window.

After double-clicking the phone icon you can use a file transfer feature to view the images stored in the phone and copy them to a folder on your computer.

Importing Images

Devices like digital cameras, dongles, etc., which connect to a USB port, can be "hot-swapped" i.e. plugged in while the computer is up and running. The USB device is detected by Windows Vista and designated as a **Removable Disk (F:)** or **(G:)**, etc. The **AutoPlay** window opens, as shown below, with options to **Import** or **View** the pictures.

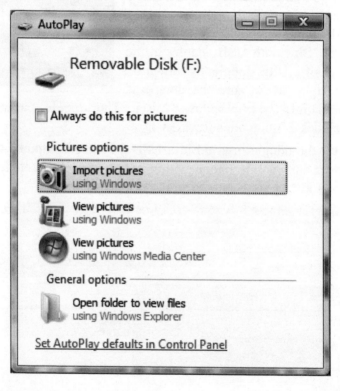

The **AutoPlay** feature is part of the Windows Vista operating system; additional software for importing images may also be supplied with a digital camera.

Click **Import pictures** shown on the previous page and you are given the option to **Tag** the images to be transferred.

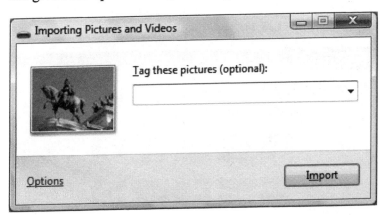

A **Tag** will allow the uploaded pictures to be displayed as a separate category or group in the **Windows Photo Gallery**. The **Gallery** may contain a library consisting of hundreds of images, so it's helpful to be able to categorise them.

Click the **Import button** shown above to start the transfer of the images.

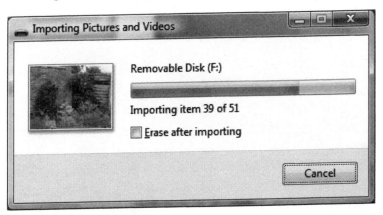

When all of the images have been transferred to the computer, the **Windows Photo Gallery** opens up, as shown below. Here you can display the entire store of photos in the **Gallery** or click a tag to display just a selection.

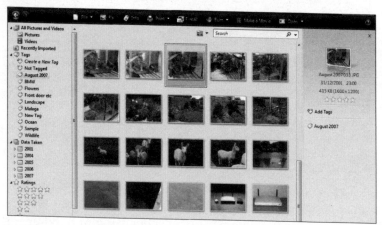

To view an individual image, double-click the image in the Windows Photo Gallery shown above. The image opens as shown below.

The Toolbar across the top of the Windows Photo Gallery has options which include printing, e-mailing and burning the image (to a CD or DVD).

Fixing an Image

The **Fix** menu has various options to improve the quality of the image, as shown on the right. **Crop Picture** allows you to remove surplus material around the outside of the image. This can be helpful in reducing the size of an image to be e-mailed or uploaded to the Internet. The area to remain after cropping is adjusted using the 8

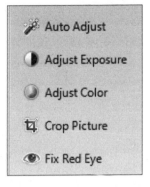

small square handles shown below. Then click **Apply** to remove the surplus material from around the outside.

Importing Images to a Folder of Your Choice

When you import pictures from a digital camera or other device, they are automatically saved in your **Pictures** folder, such as C:**\users\jim\pictures** for example. To import them to a different folder of your choice, from the Windows Photo Gallery select **File**, **Options** and click the **Import** tab.

Now click **Browse...** to search for and select the folder in which to save your imported pictures, then click **OK**.

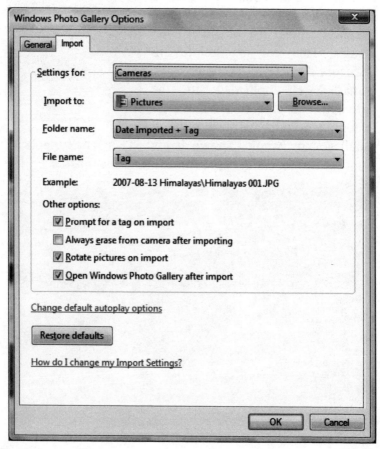

Opening Imported Images in the Pictures Folder

You can quickly access your **Pictures** folder by clicking **Start** and then **Pictures** from the main **Start** menu.

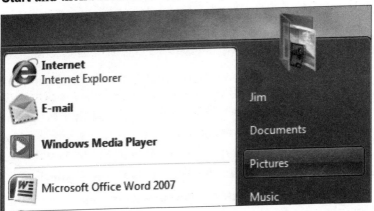

The **Pictures** folder opens as shown below. Here you can carry out all of the usual tasks needed to manage your photographs. Double-click a folder as shown below to view individual photographs. Right-click an individual photo to carry out tasks such as deleting, renaming, copying, printing, or editing a photo in the Windows Photo Gallery.

E-mailing Photographs

Photos can be e-mailed directly from the Windows Photo Gallery. You can also e-mail pictures directly from any of the folders on your hard disc, such as the **Pictures** folder just discussed.

Default Mail Program

To e-mail photos directly you must have a mail program such as **Windows Mail**, set as your *default mail program*. To do this click the **Start** button, then select **Default Programs** and **Set your default programs**. Then select **Windows Mail** (or another mail program) and **Set this program as default**.

Selecting Images from the Windows Photo Gallery

Select **Start** and **Windows Photo Gallery**, and single-click the photo(s) to be e-mailed. To select multiple images hold down the **Ctrl** key and click each image to be mailed.

From the Toolbar across the top of the **Windows Photo Gallery**, click **E-mail** as shown below.

The **Attach Files** window opens as shown below.

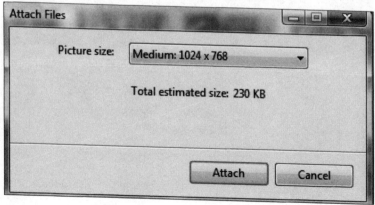

Selecting Images from a Folder on the Hard Disc

If you want to send photos from a folder on your hard disc, (other than the **Pictures** folder used by the **Photo Gallery** discussed earlier) right-click the **Start** button at the bottom left of the screen and click **Explore** from the menu which pops up. Then browse to find the folder in which your photos are stored. Now right-click over the icon for the photo and click **Mail Recipient** from the **Send To** menu.

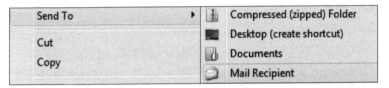

The **Attach Files** window opens as shown previously.

Reducing the Size of an Image Before E-mailing

The **Attach Files** window on the previous page shows the **Total estimated size** of the picture. Some mail servers place a limit of 1 – 2MB per message. You can adjust the size of the image by clicking the downward pointing arrow to the right of the **Picture size** slot. This method reduces the number of pixels in the image to be e-mailed – but does not affect the size of original copy saved on your hard disc.

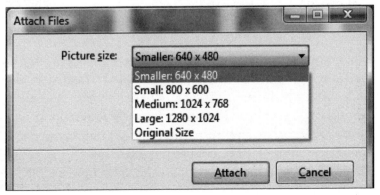

When you click the **Attach** button your e-mail program opens with the photo named in the **Attach** slot.

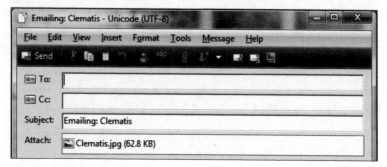

It's now just a case of completing the **To** and **Subject** fields and entering the e-mail text. Then click the **Send** button to dispatch the e-mail and attached photo(s) on their journey.

Resolution Versus Image Quality

As a test I e-mailed a JPEG photo to myself; first at the **Original Size** of 448KB (1600x1200 pixels resolution) just as it had been transferred from the camera. Then I changed the resolution to 640x480 pixels, using the **Attach Files** window as shown earlier. This reduced the size of the image to 62.8KB. This low-resolution image, when downloaded to the Windows Mail **Inbox**, was still clear and of a good enough quality for viewing on the Internet; in addition it will download much faster and take far less storage space when e-mailed and saved.

When you reduce the size of an image for sending by e-mail, the size of the original image is not affected in the folder in which it is stored. These higher resolution originals will be needed to produce any high quality prints, for example. Also, low resolution images quickly become "pixelated" if you try to enlarge them and print larger images. Individual pixels or squares then become visible.

Creating a Simple Web Site

Introduction

A Web site consists of one or more pages of information stored on a special computer known as an Internet *server*, allowing access by millions of people all over the world. Web pages usually contain text and pictures but may also include other features such as links to other pages, buttons, menus, order forms, sound recordings, animations and video clips. Sophisticated but easy-to-use programs are now available which simplify the creation of Web pages, similar in some ways to desktop publishing.

This chapter gives an overview of three ways of establishing your own presence on the World Wide Web:

The "Blog" or Online Diary

A blog or "Web log" is a journal into which you can enter text and pictures. It's very simple to create since all formatting and uploading to the Internet are done for you.

The GeoCities Online Web Page Builder

Yahoo! GeoCities provides ready-made design templates and online tools to simplify the creation of a Web site.

Serif WebPlus

This is a reasonably priced and easy-to-use Web design program, capable of producing professional looking results.

The Blog or Online Diary

One of the best known programs is Blogger, created in 1999. If you log on to **www.blogger.com** you are given very simple on-screen instructions for creating your own blog.

First you enter details such as a name for your blog and your e-mail address. Since a blog is a very simple Web site you are asked to enter the URL (Uniform Resource Locator). This is the unique Web address of your blog.

http://[   ].blogspot.com   You and others will use this to read and link to your blog.

The address of your blog will be something like **yourname.blogspot.com** if this has not already been used. This will allow other people, such as friends and family, to connect to your site and see your latest news or opinions.

During the setup process you are given a choice of twelve Web page designs or templates on which to base your blog.

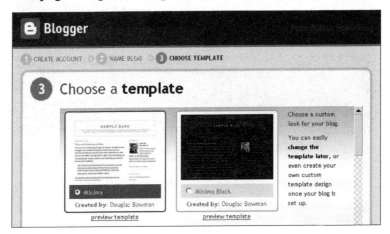

Then you're ready to start *posting* or entering the text of the blog, using the **Posting** tab in the Blogger window shown below. This has many of the features of a word-processor, including text in different styles and sizes, bold, italic, bullets, numbering and a spelling checker.

As shown below, you can insert a picture into a blog.

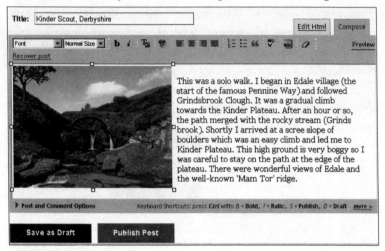

When you've finished entering the text and any pictures click **Publish Post** to upload your blog to the Internet.

The Blog – key points

- A blog is an online diary, journal or Web log.
- A blog can be used to disseminate news and information to a worldwide audience.
- A blog is a simple Web site with its own address.
- Blog software is free, online and very easy to use.
- Text, pictures and hyperlinks may be included.
- Ready-made page design templates are provided.
- A blog grows as daily or regular postings are added.
- You can allow other people to post their comments.
- You can view the blogs of lots of other people.
- The blog can be used for any legitimate purpose, but can be closed down if it is offensive, etc.

Yahoo! GeoCities

Yahoo! is one of the major providers of news and information on the Internet, with extensive directories and search facilities. GeoCities is a Yahoo! Web site which provides all of the tools needed to create your own Web site online, i.e. while you are connected to the Internet. This is one of the quickest and easiest ways to create a personal Web site – a Web page can literally be online in minutes. Some of the main features of GeoCities are:

- A range of packages costing various amounts, from a free Web page carrying advertising to subscription packages having more facilities and no advertising.

- Your own Web address, user ID and password.

- PageWizards which guide you, step-by-step, through the process of building a Web page.

- A choice of Web page templates which can be customized to include your own text and pictures.

- Web page creation software allowing you to design and create your own site starting from a blank page.

- Software and tools provided free online – all you need is a computer and Internet connection.

Getting Started with GeoCities

Log on to the Yahoo! site at **www.yahoo.com**. This opens up the main **Yahoo! Directory**, with a link to **GeoCities** on the left-hand side. Clicking the **GeoCities** link on the left opens up a welcome screen. This includes links to pages giving details of the various GeoCities packages – **Free**, **Plus** and **Pro**. If you click the link **Learn more** you can take the **Yahoo! GeoCities Tour**, which goes through the various steps in creating and publishing a Web site with **GeoCities**.

There is also a **GeoCities 360 Blog** feature allowing you to quickly create an online diary or Web log. The blog can be used to broadcast your news and opinions to a worldwide community and to receive comments back from the blogging community, similar to the Blogger online diary discussed earlier in this chapter.

There are two ways of creating Web pages in GeoCities; the **Yahoo! PageBuilder** and the **Yahoo! PageWizards**.

The **Yahoo! PageBuilder** starts off with a blank page and allows you to add your own text and images using various tools, similar to desktop publishing. This blank sheet approach is discussed shortly using another Web page design program, Serif WebPlus10.

Yahoo! PageWizards is a very quick and easy way to create stylish Web pages. The PageWizard "holds your hand" while you customize a ready-made template – similar to "painting by numbers". Each of the pieces of text (or pictures) in a Web page template are numbered. Under the guidance of the PageWizard, you replace each of the numbered pieces with your own text or picture.

Before creating your first Web page, you need to enter a few personal details and create your Yahoo! ID and password. The Yahoo! ID is used to create the address of your new Web site, for example:

http://geocities.com/jillaustin/

If Jill's friends or family wanted to view her new GeoCities Web site they would simply type the above address into the Address Bar of their Web browser, such as Internet Explorer 7, also discussed on page 131.

GeoCities PageWizards

After signing in to GeoCities, click **Create & Update** on the **Control Panel** shown below then click **Yahoo! PageWizards**.

You are presented with a set of **Quick Start** designs as shown in the sample below; these can be customized by inserting your own words and pictures to replace those in the template.

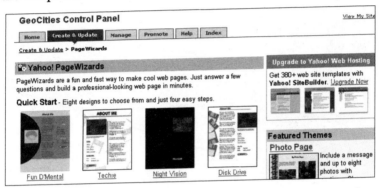

Another set of templates is based on specific themes for different events, etc., as shown in the sample below.

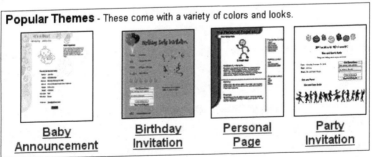

When you've chosen a template, select **Create new page** and then choose from a number of styles based on different colour schemes and layouts.

219

Entering the Page Content in the PageWizard

After choosing a template, it's time to start work by entering a title for the Web page and replacing the template text with your own content.

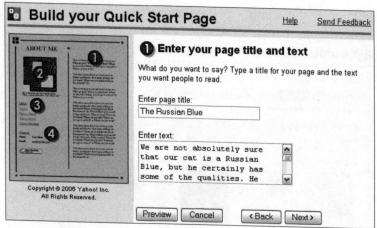

Text is entered in the box provided; the number on the main panel on the centre right of the page above corresponds to a number on the miniature Web page shown on the left-hand side. Click **Next** to move through the numbers on the page shown above.

Pictures can be inserted into a Web page using the PageWizard; click **Next** to highlight the picture, then click **Upload new image....** Now browse the hard disc to locate the picture then upload it to GeoCities. It's also possible to add hyperlinks to your Web page; some links are suggested by GeoCities such as **Yahoo! Photos**, an online photo album. You can also add links to other Web sites of your choice by typing their Web address into the bar provided.

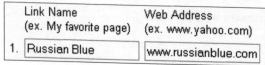

Finally after clicking **Next** again, you are required to enter a name for the Web page, such as **mypage.htm** or **mypage.html**. (Both **.htm** and **.html** can be used). To view your page, visitors simply enter your Web address into the Address Bar of their Web browser. Then up pops your Web page, like the one shown below.

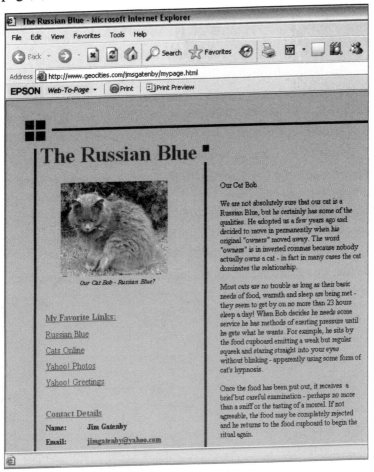

Serif WebPlus

Serif have a reputation for producing high-quality software which is easy to use. WebPlus is a package for designing professional standard Web pages and publishing the finished Web site on the Internet. WebPlus (currently under £60) is only a fraction of the cost of other Web design packages. For more details about buying WebPlus, you could have a look at the Serif (Europe) Ltd Web site at:

www.serif.com.

At the time of writing, WebPlus10 is available. However, Serif offer some earlier versions of their software completely free. For example, a free download of WebPlus 6 is available from:

www.freeserifsoftware.com

Downloading a copy of WebPlus 6 to your computer would allow you to practise many of the skills of Web site creation. In WebPlus the Web site is designed and saved locally on your own computer; then when the site is complete it is uploaded to the Internet and tested.

When you start WebPlus 10, the following menu appears.

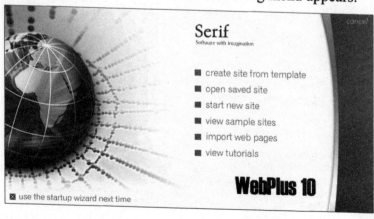

The first option on the previous menu, **create site from template**, presents a selection of some 30 page designs.

Flower Shop   Garden Centre   Health Care

Each page design is made up of a number of frames, each containing text or a picture. Frames can be individually selected and edited. The "dummy" text in a frame can be deleted and replaced by your own words. If the frame contains a picture, the **Insert** option allows you to browse for a picture from your hard disc and insert it in the frame.

Another option on the previous menu, **view sample sites**, allows you to have a look at some existing Web sites that were created using WebPlus. These include small business Web sites and a blog created using WebPlus graphics tools.

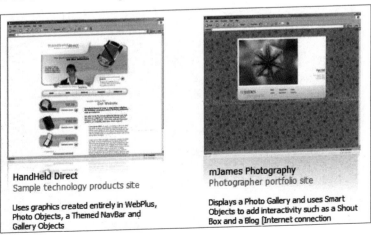

HandHeld Direct
Sample technology products site

Uses graphics created entirely in WebPlus, Photo Objects, a Themed NavBar and Gallery Objects

mJames Photography
Photographer portfolio site

Displays a Photo Gallery and uses Smart Objects to add interactivity such as a Shout Box and a Blog [Internet connection

One of the strengths of WebPlus is the large range of tools available to create your own Web site from scratch, using a "blank canvas" approach. These tools allow you to insert all of the usual desktop publishing text and graphics effects. In addition, amongst other things, you can insert into a Web page animated banners, clickable buttons and sound and video clips. If your Web site is to be used for any sort of sales, there are E-Commerce tools to insert ready-made order forms. You can also set up a PayPal account enabling customers to pay by credit card.

The screenshot below shows part of the main design window in WebPlus 10. Across the top and down the left-hand side are the various menus and tools for inserting and editing text, pictures, hyperlinks and multimedia, etc.

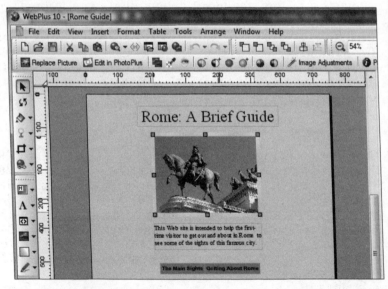

WebPlus 10 includes extensive and helpful tutorials covering all aspects of using the software, accessed by selecting **view tutorials** on the menu shown on page 222.

Index

Further Reading

If you've enjoyed reading this book and found it helpful, you may also wish to read the companion volume, **Computing with Vista for the Older Generation**, illustrated below.

Babani Computer Books

Computing with Vista for the Older Generation

- You can learn to use a computer at any age.
- Especially written for the over 50's, using plain English and avoiding technical jargon.
- Large clear type for easy reading.
- Gives you the confidence to further develop your computing skills.
- Amongst the many practical and useful ideas for using your PC that are covered in this book are:
  - ~ Choosing, setting up and understanding your computer and its main components.
  - ~ Appreciating the new features in Windows Vista.
  - ~ Getting your computer ready for Vista, installing the software and starting to use it.
  - ~ Writing letters, producing leaflets etc., using the latest Office 2007 word processor, Microsoft Word.
  - ~ Keeping track of your spending by using the latest Office 2007 spreadsheet, Microsoft Excel.
  - ~ Looking after your work by making 'backup' copies, organizing it into folders and checking for viruses.
  - ~ Using the Internet to find useful information, and using e-mail to keep in touch with family and friends.
  - ~ Using the Windows Media Player to listen to your favourite music.
  - ~ Using Windows Vista to help people with impaired vision, mobility and hearing.

✓ Beginners   ✓ Older Generation

BP 614

£7·99

ISBN 978-0-85934-614-6
00799>

9 780859 346146